Flash™ 8

Accelerated

Y.

Flash™ 8 Accelerated

ISBN: 981-05-3849-9

How to contact us

support@youngjin.com
feedback@youngjin.com.sg
Fax: 65-6339-1403

Credits

Author: Sas Jacobs
Editor: Bill Cassel
Book Designer: Litmus
Cover Designer: Chang-uk Lee
Indexer: Kori Lee

Flash™ 8

Accelerated

YJ IP Publishing Team

c o n t e n t s

Chapter | 1

Exploring the Flash 8 Workspace

The first chapter is a warm-up to prepare you for your Flash 8 adventure. For beginners who want to learn the basics quickly, this chapter offers a quick introduction to Flash and some hands-on exercises. For designers and programmers, there's a section on the new features in Flash 8 so you can get up to speed in no time.

An Introduction to Flash 8

F lash is a powerful software tool for creating multimedia content. It has grown from a simple animation package into a tool that can be used to build complete software applications. Flash 8 comes as part of the Macromedia Studio 8 family and includes several new features specifically aimed at designers.

Why Should You Use Flash 8?

Flash is a very versatile software package that offers many benefits to both designers and programmers. Some of the advantages of using Flash in your work are as follows:

- Flash mainly uses vector graphics, which allow for small file sizes and high-quality images. Flash 8 also permits you to work with bitmaps, which increase Flash Player speed. This enables you to use the best features of both types of image.
- The Flash Player plug-in is widely distributed, which makes it possible to watch Flash movies on just about any computer. Other types of devices, such as cell phones and PDAs, can play Flash movies as well.
- The program has a user-friendly interface aimed at both designers and programmers.
- Flash 8 allows you to include content from databases and XML files in your movies. It also enables you to work with multimedia and includes enhanced features for working with video.

What Can You Do with Flash?

You can use Flash to create many different types of output, including:

- Animations (including cartoons and banner advertising)
- Web sites
- Games
- Applications

Differences Between Flash Basic 8 and Flash Professional 8

Most people using Flash will benefit from using the Professional edition of Flash 8. Flash Basic 8, which doesn't have all of the features of Flash Professional 8, is aimed at designers who infrequently use Flash in their work.

Flash Professional 8 includes the following features that aren't available in Flash Basic 8:

- Additional user interface (UI) and data components
- Filters and blends
- Flash Video Encoder and advanced video options
- Advanced easing controls
- Support for Flash Lite for mobile devices

You can find out more about the differences at the Adobe Web site (http://www.adobe.com/products/flash/basic).

The Top 10 New Features in Flash 8

1. Workspace

Flash 8 includes several changes to the Workspace, including an expanded Pasteboard area around the Stage, reorganization of the Tools panel, an enhanced Color Picker that includes an alpha setting, and a reorganized Properties panel.

The Properties panel has been reorganized in Flash 8.

There are also changes to the Actions and Library panels, and you can now group like panels together.

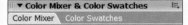

Flash 8 allows you to group related panels together into panel sets.

2. Drawing

Flash 8 introduces a new drawing mode called the Object Drawing model. In earlier versions of Flash, drawing a shape over another shape would automatically merge the two unless the shapes were drawn on different layers. In Flash 8, you can continue to draw this way or you can use the Object Drawing model to prevent the shapes from merging.

Overlapping objects drawn without the Object Drawing model merge.

Overlapping objects don't merge when you use the Object Drawing model.

3. Gradients

In Flash 8, you can add up to 15 color points when you create a gradient, and you can apply gradients to both strokes and fills. You can also double-click a point on the gradient bar to edit the color. Flash 8 includes additional options for how areas within an object that aren't completely filled by a gradient will be treated.

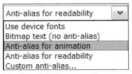

You can define up to 15 different colors along the gradient bar.

Flash 8 allows you to set a different gradient for both the stroke and the fill.

4. Text

Flash 8 includes a new text-rendering engine called FlashType that creates high-quality text, especially for small font sizes. You can also set additional anti-aliasing options in the Properties panel. Flash Professional allows you to apply your own custom anti-aliasing settings to text.

The Properties panel offers different choices for anti-aliasing.

5. Custom Easing (Flash Professional Only)

Custom easing controls give you greater control over the way animations play in your Flash movies. You can access this feature by creating a tween and clicking the Edit button in the Properties panel.

Flash 8 Professional offers custom easing controls.

You set custom easing by changing the shape of the easing graph. You can either do this for all properties at the same time, or create different graph shapes for the position, rotation, scale, color, and filters within the animation.

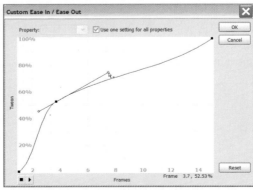

You can modify your animations by changing the shape of the custom easing graph.

6. Filters (Flash Professional Only)

Flash Professional 8 ships with seven filters: Bevel, Drop Shadow, Glow, Blur, Gradient Glow, Gradient Blur, and Adjust Color. You can apply one or more filters to movie clips, buttons, and text fields. Each filter has its own settings that can be applied through the Filters tab in the Properties panel.

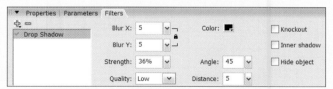

Settings for the Drop Shadow filter in the Properties panel

7. Blend Modes (Flash Professional Only)

If you've used software packages like Photoshop or Fireworks, you'll be familiar with the concept of blend modes. When images overlap one another, you can determine how the pixels interact by choosing a blend mode. Flash Professional 8 includes the following blend modes: Normal, Darken, Multiply, Lighten, Screen, Overlay, Hard Light, Add, Subtract, Difference, Invert, Alpha, and Layer. You can set the blend mode by choosing from the Blend drop-down box in the Properties panel.

Set blend mode from the Blend drop-down box in the Properties panel.

8. Bitmap Features (Flash Professional Only)

Flash Professional 8 includes some additional features for working with bitmaps: Bitmap Smoothing, which improves the appearance of bitmap images that are resized within Flash; Runtime Bitmap Caching, which enables you to set a background image as a bitmap so that the Flash Player does not have to redraw it in each frame; and ActionScript, a useful tool for creating and working with bitmap images.

9. Video (Flash Professional Only)

Flash Professional 8 includes an additional program called the Flash 8 Video Encoder. This standalone program allows you to convert video files into Flash Video Format (FLV) in batches, leaving you free to do other work.

Flash Professional 8 includes a new video codec called the On2 VP6 codec that you can use if you're publishing to Flash Player 8. There are also changes to the Video Import Wizard.

You can encode video easily with the Flash 8 Video Encoder.

10. Flash Player 8

Flash 8 includes Flash Player 8 to play SWF files. The player has been updated to support the new features in Flash 8. You can find out more about Flash Player 8 at http://www. adobe.com/products/flashplayer/.

Installing Flash 8

T he supplementary CD-ROM in the back of this book contains a trial version of Flash 8 that can be used for 30 days. You can also download the software from the Adobe Web site (http://www.adobe.com). This section provides instructions for installing the English edition of the trial version.

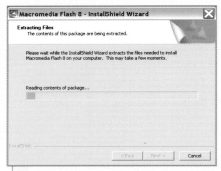

1 Open the folder containing the trial program and double-click the appropriate installation file to start the installation process. You should see the dialog box shown here while Flash extracts the relevant installation files.

2 You'll see this welcome message at the start of the installation process. Click the Next button to proceed.

3 Before you can start installing, you'll be asked to accept the license agreement. Select "I accept the terms in the license agreement" and click Next.

4 In the next step, you will decide where to install the program. Click Next to install Flash in the default location or use the Change button to choose a different location. You can also choose whether to create shortcuts at the same time.

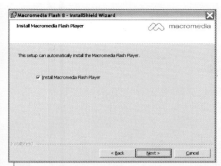

5 You will then be asked if you would like to install the Flash Player. This is generally advisable, so unless you have a reason to do otherwise, leave the box checked and click Next.

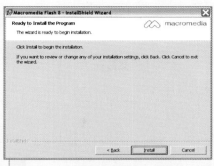

6 You are now ready to start the installation. Click Next to begin installing Flash.

7 During installation, Flash will show the above message.

8 When the installation has finished, you will see this message. Click the Finish button to close the dialog box.

The Flash 8 Interface

T his section will show you how to start Flash 8 and how to close it down when you're finished. We'll then walk you through the different elements of the Flash 8 interface. Throughout the rest of the book, we will interchangeably use the terms movie, file, and document to refer to a Flash file.

Starting Flash

1 To start Flash in Windows, choose Start > Programs or Start > All Programs and select Macromedia > Macromedia Flash 8.

2 You'll be asked whether you want to buy or try the software. Choose "I want to try Macromedia Flash" and click Continue.

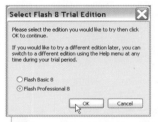

3 The next dialog box asks you which version of Flash you would like to try. Choose "Flash Professional 8" and click OK.

4 Flash 8 will start and the Start Page will appear. Click Flash Document in the Create New section to start working with a new Flash movie.

tip >>

Switching Trial Versions

When evaluating the trial edition of Flash Professional 8, you can switch to the Basic version at any time by choosing Help > Try Flash Basic 8. When you purchase Flash, this option won't be available to you.

Shutting Down Flash

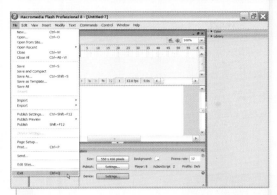

Save on Exit

If you have any unsaved documents when you choose File > Exit, you will be prompted to save them. The next chapter will go into detail about how to save your work.

1 To close down Flash, choose File > Exit from the menu bar at the top of the screen.

Understanding the Flash Interface

When you first open Flash, the Workspace can seem a little daunting. The aim of this part of the book is to familiarize you with the different elements that you'll see onscreen.

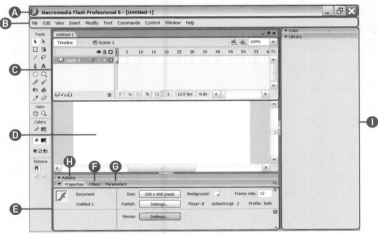

The Flash interface showing a new movie

Ⓐ Title bar: The title bar shows the name of the software and the title of the current movie.

Ⓑ Menu bar: The menu bar is one way to access Flash's commands, which are organized here into relevant sections. Many of the commands are available in other parts of Flash or by using shortcuts.

Ⓒ Timeline: The Timeline shows the structure of the Flash movie, divided into frames. It is used to control and edit the timing of animations.

Ⓓ Stage: One way to understand Flash is to treat each movie as a play made up of objects (actors) appearing on a stage. The Stage is the location for the objects that you want to animate.

15

ⓔ Properties: The Properties panel shows the properties of the currently selected object. If nothing is selected, the properties of the document are displayed.

ⓕ Filters: The Filters tab is available only in Flash Professional 8. It allows you to add and modify filters.

ⓖ Parameters: The Parameters tab in the Properties panel applies only to components. It shows the parameters for whichever component is currently selected on the Stage.

ⓗ Actions: The Actions panel shows any ActionScript that has been added to a movie.

ⓘ Other Panels: Flash contains a number of other panels that you can use when creating and editing a movie. These panels will be covered in more detail later in the chapter.

The Timeline

The Timeline shows the structure of your movie, divided into frames. To continue the stage play analogy, the Timeline is a diagram of all of the acts in the play, indicating which actors are onstage at any given time and what they are doing.

Learning to use the Timeline is an essential part of working with Flash. The Timeline includes the frames and layers that make up a Flash movie and you will use it constantly when creating and editing movies. Whenever you click on a different part of the Timeline, the frame that you select will appear on the Stage below.

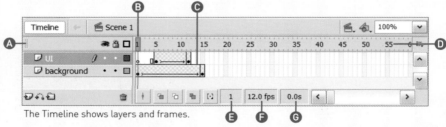

The Timeline shows layers and frames.

ⓐ Layers: Layers will be familiar to people who use Photoshop. They can be thought of as transparent sheets that contain the contents of your movie. Layers allow you to control the way objects overlap in the movie.

ⓑ Playhead: The Playhead is a red pointer that moves through each frame in sequence as a Flash movie is played. You can drag it along the Timeline to view your animation or select a new frame.

ⓒ Frames: All animations are made up of frames played in a certain order. The frame is the smallest unit of a movie, and each is numbered, starting at 1. There are different types of frames in Flash; we will cover this in detail later in the book.

ⓓ Timeline Header: The Timeline header shows the frame numbers as well as the position of the Playhead.

ⓔ Current Frame Position: This box shows the frame number where the Playhead is currently located.

ⓕ Play Speed: This box shows the movie's frame rate. Each movie has its own frame rate measured in frames per second (fps). At 12 fps, every 12 frames will take one second to play. The higher the frame rate, the more frames are played each second and the faster the movie will run.

G **Play Time**: The play time shows how much time it will take to play the movie up to the Playhead. If the Playhead is at the beginning of the movie, the play time will show 0.0s.

The Tools Panel

The Tools panel is Flash's own Swiss Army knife. It contains 18 different tools that do everything from creating shapes and lines to adding text and even transforming your graphics and gradients. Learning to use these tools is essential to creating Flash movies.

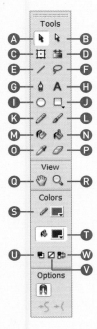

A Ⓐ **Selection Tool**: The Selection tool selects and moves objects in your movies. Press V on the keyboard to bring up this tool.

B Ⓑ **Subselection Tool**: This tool is used to modify the border of an object or change its shape. To access it, press the letter A on the keyboard.

C Ⓒ **Free Transform Tool**: The Free Transform tool modifies the size, rotation, and distortion of objects. Activate it by pressing Q on the keyboard.

D Ⓓ **Gradient Transform Tool**: The Gradient Transform tool changes the size and direction of the gradient filling an object. Press F on the keyboard to activate this tool.

E Ⓔ **Line Tool**: The Line tool draws straight lines and can be activated by pressing N on the keyboard.

F Ⓕ **Lasso Tool**: This tool enables you to create irregularly shaped selections in a movie. Press L on the keyboard to activate it.

G Ⓖ **Pen Tool**: The Pen tool creates paths and anchor points for drawing curves or straight lines. Photoshop users will be familiar with this tool; others will need a little practice to get the hang of it. Press P to use the Pen tool.

H Ⓗ **Text Tool**: The Text tool adds text to a movie. Press T brings up this tool.

I 🔘 **Oval Tool:** The Oval tool draws oval and circular shapes and can be activated by pressing O on the keyboard.

J 🔳 **Rectangle Tool:** This tool draws square and rectangular shapes. If you click and hold down the left mouse button on this tool, you'll open a menu that allows you to switch to the PolyStar tool, which draws polygons and stars. Both tools can be accessed by pressing the letter R on the keyboard.

K ✏️ **Pencil Tool:** The Pencil tool draws freeform lines and can be activated by pressing Y on the keyboard.

L 🖌️ **Brush Tool:** The Brush tool simulates drawing with a paint brush. You can vary the size and tip shape of the brush according to your needs. Access this tool by pressing B on the keyboard.

M 🍶 **Ink Bottle Tool:** The Ink Bottle tool adds a border or changes the color of an existing border. Press S on the keyboard to use this tool.

N 🪣 **Paint Bucket Tool:** The Paint Bucket tool enables you to fill an object with color or change the existing color of an object. This tool can be activated by pressing K on the keyboard.

O 💧 **Eyedropper Tool:** The Eyedropper tool lets you duplicate a color onscreen by clicking on it. To select the Eyedropper tool, press the I key.

P ⬜ **Eraser Tool:** The Eraser tool is used to erase parts of objects. Press the E key to activate it.

Q ✋ **Hand Tool:** The Hand tool drags the Stage so that you can see hidden parts of your movie. Press H on the keyboard to bring up this tool.

R 🔍 **Zoom Tool:** The Zoom tool zooms in or out of the Stage. You can access the Zoom tool by pressing either M or Z.

S 🖊️ **Stroke Color Tool:** The Stroke Color tool brings up a Color Picker that allows you to choose the color of a line.

T 🪣 **Fill Color Tool:** The Fill Color tool lets you choose the fill color of an object.

U 🔲 **Black and White Button:** This button allows you to return the line and fill colors to their default settings (i.e., the line color is black and the fill color is white).

V ◻️ **No Color Button:** This button indicates that no color has been selected.

W 🔳 **Swap Colors Button:** Clicking this button swaps the selected line and fill colors.

The Properties Panel

The Properties panel shows you the properties of any object that you have selected. The panel changes each time you select a new tool or object. If nothing is selected, the panel displays the properties of the document.

Document Properties

When nothing is selected, the Properties panel shows the properties of the document, including the size of the movie, the background color, and the frame rate.

The Properties panel showing the document settings

Text Properties

When the Text tool is selected, the Properties panel displays text properties such as font, font size, color, and alignment.

Text properties displayed in the Properties panel

Object Properties

When you select an object that you have drawn in Flash, the Properties panel shows the height, width, and X and Y positions of the object. It also allows you to change the line and fill colors and line thickness.

The Properties panel showing settings for an object

Frame Properties

When you select a frame in the Timeline, the Properties panel shows frame properties. You can create animations and insert sounds from within this panel.

Properties of a frame

Symbol Properties

Flash allows you to save repeated or reused graphical objects as symbols; this provides for a faster workflow and better performance in your animations. When you select a symbol, properties such as the position of the symbol and the type of symbol are displayed in the Properties panel.

The Properties panel showing symbol properties

Panels in Flash 8

F lash 8's Window menu includes several panels to help you work with movies. You can hide and show panels by choosing them from this menu or by using their shortcut keys. You'll notice that each of the panels appears within a group in the menu.

Common Panels

The first set of panels includes the Timeline, Tools, Properties, Library, and Common Libraries panels. We've already covered most of these, but let's take a quick look at the Library and Common Libraries panels.

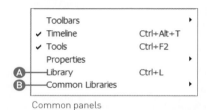

Common panels

Ⓐ Library: The Library panel shows the symbols that are contained in a movie. You can access it with the Ctrl-L shortcut (Command-L for Macintosh).

Ⓑ Common Libraries: The Common Libraries panel contains symbols such as buttons that come free with Flash 8.

The Common Libraries included with Flash 8

The Library panel

Developer Panels

The second set of panels includes panels specifically aimed at developers or programmers.

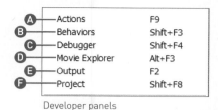

Ⓐ	Actions	F9
Ⓑ	Behaviors	Shift+F3
Ⓒ	Debugger	Shift+F4
Ⓓ	Movie Explorer	Alt+F3
Ⓔ	Output	F2
Ⓕ	Project	Shift+F8

Developer panels

Ⓐ **Actions**: The Actions panel is used to add ActionScript to a movie. It appears above the Properties panel and can be accessed with the F9 key.

The Actions panel

Ⓑ **Behaviors**: The Behaviors panel allows you to add actions to your movie without writing ActionScript. Behaviors can range from simple actions like linking to a Web page or playing a sound to very complicated actions, such as triggering a data source. This panel can be accessed with the shortcut Shift-F3.

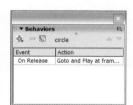

The Behaviors panel

Ⓒ **Debugger**: The Debugger panel is used for finding and fixing ActionScript errors. Press Shift-F4 to show this panel.

The Debugger panel

Ⓓ **Movie Explorer**: The Movie Explorer panel shows all of the graphics, objects, and components that have been used in the movie. The Movie Explorer panel can be accessed with the Alt-F3 shortcut (Option-F3 for Macintosh).

The Movie Explorer panel

E **Output**: The Output panel is used by programmers to list trace and debugger actions. Press F2 to display this panel.

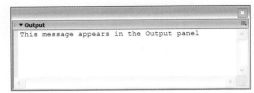

The Output panel

F **Project**: The Project panel is included with Flash Professional 8. It is used to create and manage Flash projects. You can display this panel using the Shift-F8 shortcut.

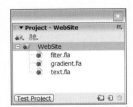

The Project panel

Designer Panels

The third group of panels is aimed at Flash designers.

A	Align	Ctrl+K
B	Color Mixer	Shift+F9
C	Color Swatches	Ctrl+F9
D	Info	Ctrl+I
E	Transform	Ctrl+T

Designer panels

A **Align**: The Align panel lets you align, arrange, and distribute objects evenly on the Stage. It appears in a group with the Info and Transform panels. The shortcut for the Align panel is Ctrl-K (Command-K for Macintosh).

The Align panel

B **Color Mixer**: This panel is used to mix colors that can be used for lines, fills, gradients, and text. It appears with the Color Swatches panel in the Color panel group. You can access the Color Mixer panel with the shortcut Shift-F9.

The Color Mixer panel

C Color Swatches: The Color Swatches panel displays blocks of color that you can use for objects in Flash. You can use this panel to save and load swatch files. The shortcut is Ctrl-F9 (Command-F9 for Macintosh).

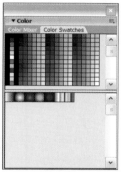

The Color Swatches panel

D Info: The Info panel displays object information such as position, size, and color. It can be accessed with the shortcut Ctrl-I (Command-I for Macintosh).

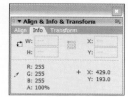

The Info panel

E Transform: The Transform panel can be used to change the size, rotation, and skew of an object and can be accessed with Ctrl-T (Command-T for Macintosh).

The Transform panel

The Components and Component Inspector Panels

The next group of panels includes the Components and Component Inspector panels.

Component panels

A Components: The Components panel contains user interface components that can be used to create applications. You can also add free and commercial third-party components. The shortcut for this panel is Ctrl-F7 (Command-F7 for Macintosh).

The Components panel

B **Component Inspector**: The Component Inspector panel shows the properties of components that are on the Stage. You can change the properties of a component by selecting it and then making the changes in the Component Inspector panel. To display the Component Inspector panel, press Alt-F7 (Option-F7 on a Macintosh).

The Component Inspector panel

Other Panels

Lastly, Flash 8 includes the following panels in the Other Panels menu.

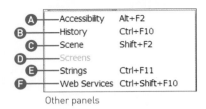

Other panels

A **Accessibility**: The Accessibility panel is used to provide text alternatives for Flash movie objects to make them accessible to people with disabilities. The shortcut for this panel is Alt-F2 (Option-F2 for Macintosh).

The Accessibility panel

B **History**: The History panel shows a list of all actions that have been carried out in the current session. The shortcut for this panel is Ctrl-F10 (Command-F10 for Macintosh).

The History panel

C **Scene**: As with a play, a Flash movie can be broken down into multiple scenes. In the Scene panel you can add, edit, and delete scenes within your movie. This panel can be displayed using the shortcut Shift-F2.

The Scene panel

ⓓ **Strings**: The Strings panel allows you to publish a movie in multiple languages. The shortcut for the Strings panel is Ctrl-F11 (Command-F11 for Macintosh).

The Strings panel

ⓔ **Web Services**: The Web Services panel manages connections to Web services. You can bring it up with the shortcut Ctrl-Shift-F10 (Command-Shift-F10 for Macintosh).

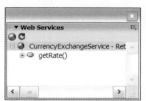

The Web Services panel

Help Panel

You can bring up the Help panel by choosing Flash Help from the Help menu or by pressing the F1 key. This panel contains all of the Flash 8 help documentation as well as tutorials, samples, and a comprehensive search function. You can update the contents of the Help panel by clicking the Update button at the top right of the panel.

The Help panel

Learning how to work with panels in Flash is very important. Because there are so many panels available, you need to strike a balance between having the panels you need open and keeping your workspace uncluttered. This section will show you how to work with panels more effectively.

Minimizing Panels

You can minimize a panel by clicking on its title, reducing the amount of space it takes up on the screen. It will change to a horizontal bar with a right-pointing arrow.

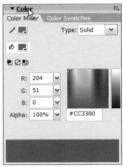

Maximizing Panels

When a panel is minimized, you can open it by clicking on the title. It will change to a full window with a downward-pointing arrow.

Clicking the title expands a minimized panel.

Clicking the title minimizes an expanded panel.

Closing Panels

To close a panel, click the Panel Options button at the right of the title bar and select the Close option. If the panel is part of a group, you can also choose the "Close panel group" option.

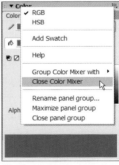

Closing a panel

Viewing the Panel Options Menu

Click the Panel Options button to show the Options menu. The menu will include options specific to the chosen panel as well as the options available to all panels.

The Panel Options pop-up menu

Hiding Panels

You can hide panels by pressing F4 or by choosing Windows > Hide Panels. The panels won't close, but they will be temporarily hidden. If there is a checkmark next to the Hide Panels menu, the panels are already hidden. Click the Hide Panels option or press F4 to view the panels again. The F4 key works as a toggle to hide and show panels.

Minimizing All Vertical and Horizontal Panels

If you need to create some more workspace, you can minimize all the horizontal and vertical panel spaces at the right and bottom of the screen. To move all the vertical panels to the right, click the arrow button in the center of the vertical panel space. When the panels are hidden, you can click this button again to restore the panels to their original positions.

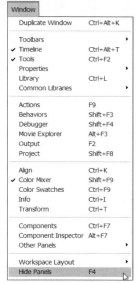

Hiding panels

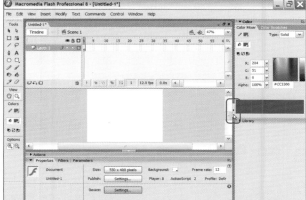

Hiding the vertical panel space

The horizontal panel space also has a central arrow button that hides the panels at the bottom of the screen. Again, once the panels are hidden, you can click the button again to move them back to their original positions.

Floating Panels

You can customize your workspace by moving panels from their docked positions to any other part of the Workspace. Panels that aren't docked are called floating panels.

To create a floating panel, click and hold down your mouse button on the left side of the panel's title bar. The mouse pointer will change to a double-headed arrow and you will be able to drag the panel to any location on the screen.

The panel will appear semi-transparent while you hold down the mouse button. If you see a solid black outline, Flash will dock the panel to the outlined position on the screen.

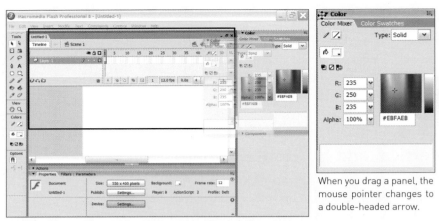

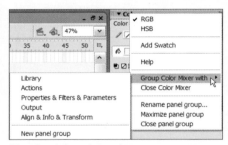

When you drag a panel, the mouse pointer changes to a double-headed arrow.

A solid black line indicates that the panel will dock to that area of the screen.

Grouping Panels

Similar panels are often grouped together so that each one appears as a tab in the same group. For example, the Color Mixer and Color Swatches panels appear in the same group.

Grouped panels

Flash 8 includes a new feature that allows you to rearrange panel groups. From the pop-up Panel menu, choose the "Group with" option and you'll see a list of existing panel groups. Select an item from the list and the current panel will be added to that group. You can also choose the "New panel group" option to create your own group.

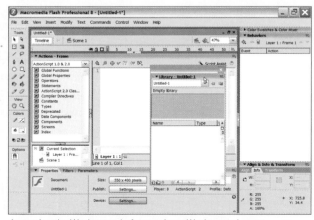

Changing the panel grouping

Creating Your Own Workspace Layout

We've covered some of the basic skills you need to use Flash and by now you should be comfortable with the standard Flash environment. You can customize the Workspace so that it suits your needs better by creating and saving your own Workspace Layout. You can even create multiple layouts and switch between them.

Start by arranging the panels and groups on the screen. You might want to open some panels that are currently closed and close others that are currently open. You may want to make some panels floating and others docked.

Arranging the Workspace before saving a Workspace Layout

You can save the current Workspace Layout by choosing Window > Workspace Layout > Save Current.

Enter a name for the layout and click OK.

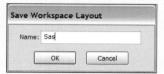

Naming the Workspace Layout

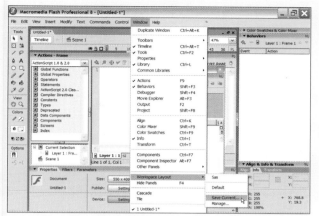

Saving the current Workspace Layout

You can test the new Workspace Layout by switching to the default layout. Choose Window > Workspace Layout > Default and the Workspace will be reset to the default layout.

Now open your customized Workspace Layout by choosing Window > Workspace Layout and selecting the name you entered earlier.

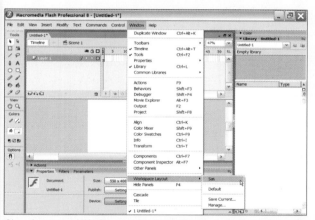

Choosing a saved Workspace Layout

The Workspace will change to show your custom Workspace Layout.

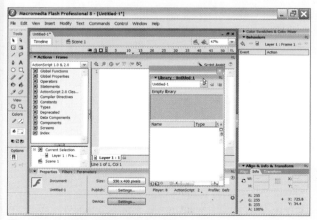

The customized Workspace Layout

Working with Flash Movies

B efore you can create animations in your Flash movies, you'll need to learn how to work with files, including opening and saving them. Saving Flash files is an important skill and one that you should practice often so you don't accidentally lose your work!

Creating a New Flash Movie

You can create a new Flash movie by selecting File > New from the menu bar and choosing Flash Document.

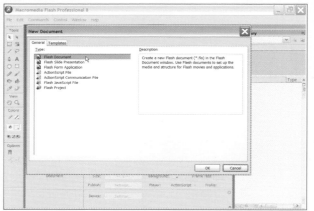

Choosing the Flash Document option from the New Document dialog box

You can also create a new movie by clicking the Flash Document option in the middle of the Start Page.

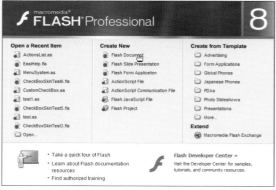

Choosing the Flash Document option from the Start Page

Before you start working on your movie, you will need to set up its height and width, as well as its background color and frame rate.

1 Create a new movie by choosing File > New and selecting Flash Document from the General tab. Click OK.

2 The Properties panel will show the document's properties.

3 Change the size of the movie by clicking the Size button or by using the Ctrl-J shortcut (Command-J on a Macintosh).

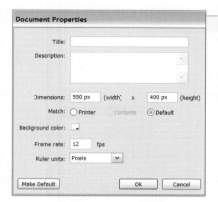

4 You'll see the Document Properties dialog box, which allows you to change the size of the movie and other settings.

5 Change the size of the movie to a width of 300 pixels and a height of 200 pixels. Click OK.

note >>>

Document Properties Dialog Box

Ⓐ Title: The title of the movie. This is metadata about the movie that can be used by search engines.

Ⓑ Description: The description of the movie. This is also metadata about the movie that can be used by search engines, so you may want to include keywords here.

Ⓒ Dimensions: The width and height of the movie in pixels.

Ⓓ Match: Sets the size of the movie to Printer, Contents, or Default. Choosing one of these options will automatically change the width and height of the movie.

Ⓔ Background color: Lets you use the Color Picker to select a background color for the movie.

Ⓕ Frame rate: Set the speed of the movie in frames per second. As this number gets higher, more frames will play in each second of your movie.

Ⓖ Ruler units: Set the units used by the ruler. You can choose from inches, inches (decimal), points, centimeters, millimeters, or pixels.

Ⓗ Make Default: Sets the current values as the defaults for future movies.

tip >>

Changing the Background Color

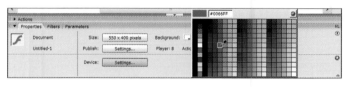

You can change the background color by clicking the Background box in the Properties panel.

It is important to get into the habit of saving your work regularly. This can help you avoid accidentally losing movies that you've put a lot of work into. It's also important to think about how you name and organize your files. Using a good naming strategy and filing system will help you find your movies later on.

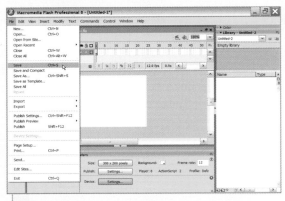

1 To save your Flash movie, choose File > Save from the menu bar.

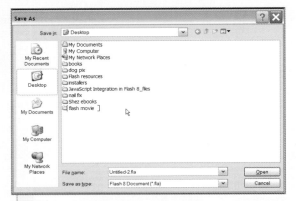

2 The first time you save a new movie, you will be asked to specify a filename and location in the Save As dialog box. Choose Desktop from the drop-down menu at the top of the window. Click the Create new folder icon and enter "flash movie" as the name of the folder.

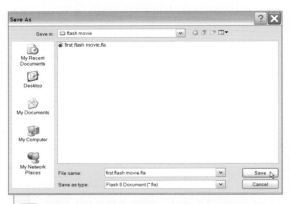

3 Double-click the "flash movie" folder, enter "first flash movie.fla" as the name of the file, and click Save.

4 When you return to your movie, the name will appear in the title bar at the top of the page as well as on the tab for the document.

The next time you save this file, you won't be asked for the name and location. If you'd like to save a copy of the movie under a different name or in a different location, choose Save As from the File menu instead of Save.

Closing a Flash Movie

To close a movie, choose File > Close from the menu bar. You can also use the Ctrl-W shortcut (Command-W on a Macintosh). To practice, close the Flash movie that you just saved.

Opening an Existing Flash Movie

You can open an existing Flash movie by selecting File > Open from the menu bar at the top of the screen.

Navigate to the folder that contains the Flash file you want, select it, and click Open. (For practice, open the file 01_001.fla from the supplementary CD-ROM.)

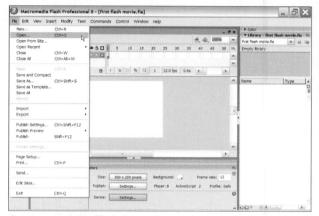

Choosing a file to open

Opening an existing Flash document

Opening Recently Used Files

You can use the Start Page to open a file that you've worked on recently. The Start Page appears each time you open Flash and whenever you have no files open. It lists the files that you have recently worked on, making it much quicker to locate them. To open a file, click its title in the Open a Recent Item section on the left of the Start Page. You can also choose File > Open Recent from the menu bar.

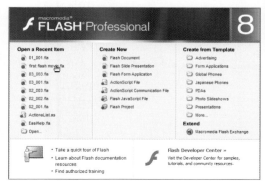

Opening a file from the Start Page

If you have several files open at the same time, the name of each file will be displayed as a tab. You can use these tabs to switch between files.

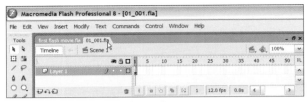

Each open movie is displayed as a tab

Testing a Movie

You can test your Flash movie by choosing Control > Test Movie or by using the Ctrl-Enter shortcut (Command-Return on a Macintosh). Testing shows you how the movie will look when it is published.

Testing a Flash movie

The movie will be displayed in a pop-up window using the Flash Player.

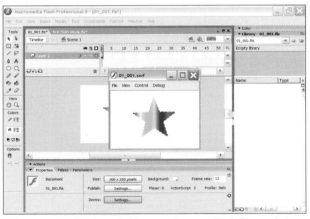

When you test a Flash movie, it appears in a new Flash Player window.

34

Publishing a Movie

Before you can share your Flash movies with other people, you will need to publish your work. This creates files that can be played with the Flash Player.

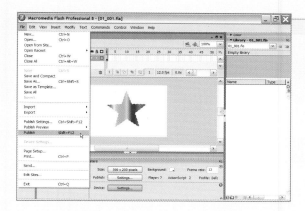

1 To publish a movie, choose File > Publish from the menu bar. Practice by publishing your "first flash movie.fla" file.

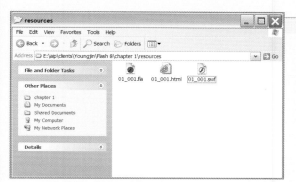

2 You can see your published files in the folder where the Flash movie is saved. Publishing creates three files, each with a different file extension. The FLA file is the file that you'll work with in Flash. The SWF file is for use with the Flash Player, while the HTML file displays the movie in a Web browser.

Minimize Flash and open the "flash movie" folder on the desktop to see the different files.

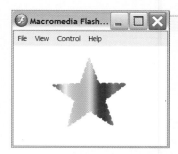

3 You can see the movie in the Flash Player by double-clicking the SWF file.

tip >>

Viewing Published Movies

Flash Player 8 is installed along with the Flash program. You can also view the movie on a Web page by double-clicking the HTML file.

Getting Comfortable with the Stage

In this section, we'll look at some of the tools you'll need to be familiar with to work with the Stage.

Using the Hand Tool

The Hand tool is used to navigate around your Flash movie and is particularly important where parts of the Stage are hidden. If you are working with another tool and want to switch to the Hand tool temporarily, simply hold down the spacebar.

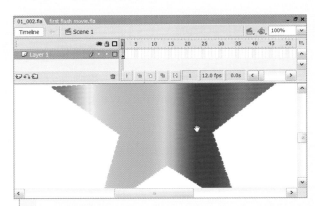

1 Select File > Open and choose the sample file 01_002.fla.

2 Choose the Hand tool (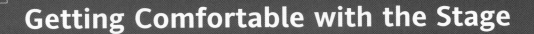) from the Tools panel. The mouse pointer will change to a hand.

2 Click and hold down the left mouse button on the picture of the star. Drag the picture upwards and release the mouse button.

Using the Zoom Tool

The Zoom tool lets you zoom into and out of the Stage.

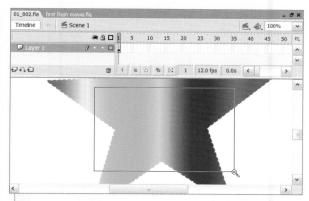

1 Choose the Zoom tool (🔍) from the View section of the Tools panel. The mouse pointer changes to a magnifying glass.

2 At the bottom of the Tools panel, in the Options section, there are two magnifying glasses, one with a plus sign 🔍 and the other with a minus sign 🔍.

3 The magnifying glass with the plus sign zooms into the movie. You can either click on the Stage or drag a selection area with the tool. The magnifying glass with the minus sign zooms out. Again, you can click or drag a selection area. Experiment with using these tools on the star image.

tip >>

Keyboard Commands for the Zoom Tool

Pressing the Z key on the keyboard activates the Zoom tool 🔍.

The Alt/Option key acts as a toggle for the Zoom tool. Holding down the Alt/Option key changes from zoom in 🔍 to zoom out 🔍. If zoom out 🔍 is selected, the Alt/Option key will switch to zoom in 🔍.

Using Shortcut Keys to Zoom
You can also zoom in or out using shortcut keys instead of the Zoom tool. Press Ctrl-+ (Crtl-plus sign) to zoom in and Ctrl-– (Ctrl-minus sign) to zoom out of the movie (Command-+ and Command-– on a Macintosh).

Using the Zoom Menu
The Zoom menu at the top right of the Timeline allows you to choose from preset percentage settings. You can also type your own value or choose Fit in Window, Show Frame, or Show All.

Chapter 2

Flash Drawing Techniques

Before you can start creating animations in Flash, you will need to draw the objects that you are going to animate. Flash comes with a set of customizable tools for this purpose, and in this chapter you will learn how to use them. In the first part of the chapter, we will look at the tools in the Tools panel and explore the options that are available for each tool. Later on, we'll cover the Arrange, Align, and Trace Bitmap menu commands, which will give you more flexibility when drawing in Flash.

Basic Drawing Tools

The basic drawing tools in Flash include the Line, Pencil, Oval, and Rectangle tools. When you draw with the Rectangle and Oval tools, you can create either a line around the outside of the shape, the fill inside the shape, or both. The Pencil and Line tools only create lines.

The Line Tool ()

The Line tool draws straight lines and can be accessed by clicking the tool or by pressing the N key on the keyboard. After selecting this tool, you can set the line color, thickness, and line type in the Properties panel.

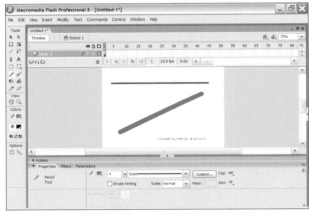

With the Line tool, you can draw lines of different colors and thicknesses.

tip >>

Drawing Horizontal, Vertical, and Diagonal Lines

Hold down the Shift key when using the Line tool to draw vertical, horizontal, and 45-degree diagonal lines.

tip >>

Cap and Join

Flash 8 allows you to draw lines of up to 200 pixels in width. It also includes new options for Cap and Join types in the Properties panel (Cap sets a style for the ends of lines, while Join determines what happens when two lines meet).

Cap types   Join types

The Oval Tool (⊙) and the Rectangle Tool (▣)

The Oval tool draws ovals and circles, while the Rectangle tool draws squares and rectangles. The Rectangle tool also includes the PolyStar tool, which creates polygons and stars. The Properties panel allows you to set the border color, thickness, and type as well as the fill color for these tools.

Using the Oval Tool (⊙)

You can access the Oval tool by pressing the letter O on the keyboard. Set the properties for the tool using the Properties panel and then click and drag on the Stage to create an oval shape. If you hold down the Shift key at the same time, you will create a circle.

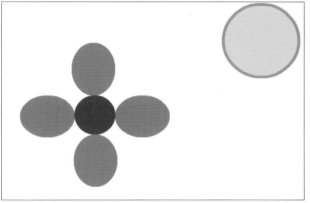

You can use the Oval tool to draw ovals and circles.

Using the Rectangle Tool (▣)

The Rectangle tool works in a similar way to the Oval tool and can be brought up with the letter R on the keyboard. After setting the properties for the tool, click and drag on the Stage to create a rectangle. If you hold down the Shift key at the same time, you will create a square.

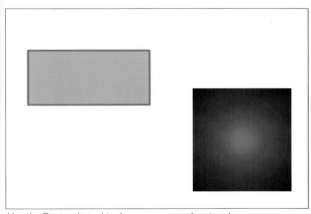

Use the Rectangle tool to draw squares and rectangles.

The Rectangle tool can also be used to draw rectangles and squares with rounded corners. Choose the Set Corner Radius button from the options section of the Tools panel to open the Rectangle Settings dialog box, then enter the desired corner radius to add rounded corners.

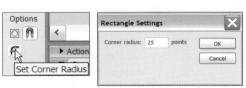

The Rectangle Settings dialog box

41

Corner radius values must be between 0 and 999. The larger the value, the more rounded the corners will be. If you make this value large enough, you can even draw a circle.

If you click and hold the Rectangle tool, a menu will appear that allows you to choose between the Rectangle tool and the PolyStar tool (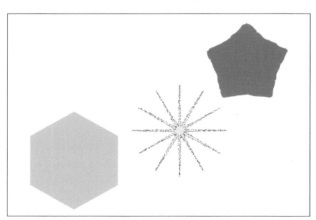), which lets you draw stars and polygons.

Choosing the PolyStar tool

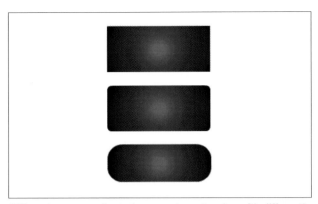

Different corner radius values create rectangles with differently rounded corners.

You can change the PolyStar tool properties from the Properties panel. In addition to the standard line and fill properties, the Option button brings up the Tool Settings dialog box with additional tool options.

The PolyStar tool settings

The Tool Settings dialog box allows you to choose the style of the tool, either polygon or star, the number of sides, and (for a star) the size of the points.

Selecting a style

By combining these options you can draw a range of different polygon and star shapes.

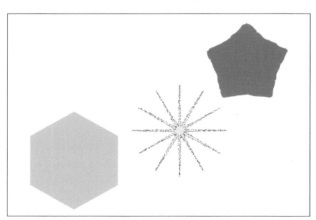

These shapes were drawn with the PolyStar tool.

tip >>

Select the Oval or Rectangle tool and Alt-click (Option-click for Macintosh) on the Stage to bring up the Oval or Rectangle Settings dialog box.

The Oval Settings dialog box   The Rectangle Settings dialog box

Free-Form Drawing Tools

The Pencil, Brush, and Erase tools enable you to draw lines, paint, and erase "by hand," as it were.

The Pencil Tool (✏️)

The Pencil tool draws free-form lines. You can access this tool with the Y key and set the line thickness, color, and type in the Properties panel.

The Pencil tool enables you to draw free-form lines.

The options section of the Tools panel contains settings that can be used to make lines smoother. There are three options: straighten, smooth, and ink.

The three Pencil tool types

- **Straighten**: Converts the line into straight segments.
- **Smooth**: Makes the lines as smooth as possible, using gentle curves.
- **Ink**: Makes the fewest changes possible to create natural-looking lines.

The Brush Tool (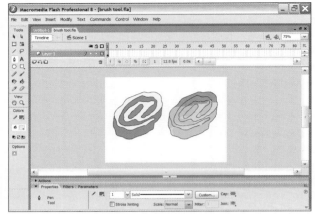)

The Brush tool, which is activated by pressing B on the keyboard, is used to apply color to objects. You can specify the brush size, shape, and color, as well as how color is to be applied.

This graphic was colored using the Brush tool.

Brush Tool Options

The Brush tool options appear in the options section of the Tools panel.

■ Brush Mode

The Brush mode determines how paint will be applied to an object.

Ⓐ Paint Normal: Paints everything.

Ⓑ Paint Fills: Paints over fills or empty spaces. Does not paint over lines.

Ⓒ Paint Behind: Paints empty spaces. Ignores objects.

Ⓓ Paint Selection: Paints selected lines and fills. Does not paint in empty spaces.

Ⓔ Paint Inside: Paints only inside the area where you started painting with the Brush tool.

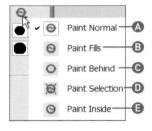

An example of each Brush mode

■ Lock Fill

When Lock Fill is selected, objects that you fill will be treated as if they were connected. This allows you to apply a single gradient to more than one object, for example.

■ Brush Size (●▾)

This lets you specify what size brush you want to use.

■ Brush Shape (■▾)

This option determines the shape of your brush.

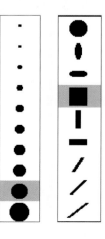

The Eraser Tool (✎)

The Eraser tool erases lines and surfaces. It comes with five different modes and can be activated by pressing E on the keyboard.

Eraser Tool Options

The Eraser tool options determine what effect the Eraser tool has on objects on the Stage.

■ Erase Mode

ⓐ Erase Normal: Erases everything.

ⓑ Erase Fills: Erases fills but ignores lines.

ⓒ Erase Lines: Erases lines but ignores fills.

ⓓ Erase Selected Fills: Erases fills inside the current selection.

ⓔ Erase Inside: Erases only inside the area where you first started erasing.

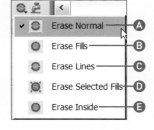

Examples of each Eraser mode

■ Faucet (🚰)

Click this to erase complicated lines and fills.

■ Erase Shape (●▾)

This option sets the shape and size of the Eraser tool.

The Text Tool (A)

The Text tool adds text to Flash files and can be activated by pressing T on the keyboard. There are three types of text that can be added to your movies: static, dynamic, and input. The dynamic and input text types are normally used for Flash programming. Use the Properties panel to adjust the font, font size, color, alignment, and spacing for your text.

The Text Tool Properties Panel

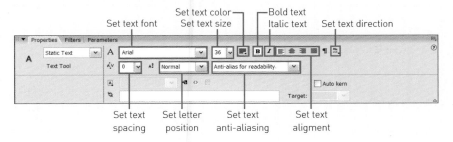

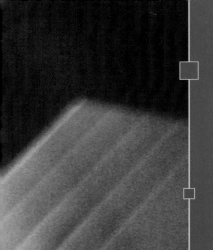

Selection and Editing Tools

If you want to edit an object drawn with the Line, Pencil, Oval, or Rectangle tools, you will have to select it first with either the Arrow or Lasso tool.

Selecting Objects Using the Arrow Tool (▍)

One way to select objects for editing is by using the Arrow tool, which you can access by pressing V on the keyboard.

Selecting Lines

For an object made up of multiple lines, clicking the tool once on the object will select the line you clicked on. If you want to select all the lines in the object, double-click and all lines connecting to the clicked line will be selected at the same time.

tip >>

Line Breaks

If there is a break in the line, you can still double-click to make a selection.

Selecting Lines and Fills

Objects created with the Oval or Rectangle tools may be made up of both a line and a fill. You can either click the fill to select just that area, or double-click the fill to select both the lines and the fill.

Making a Selection by Dragging

You can also drag the Selection tool to create a selection. Click and hold the mouse outside the object and drag it around the object. You will notice a selection outline. When you release the mouse, the area inside the outline will be selected. You can use this technique to select a whole object or even part of an object.

Making Multiple Selections and Undoing Selections

You can add to your original selection by holding down the Shift key when you make the next selection. You can also deselect an area that has already been selected by holding down the Shift key when you click on it.

Using the Selection Tool to Change an Object's Shape

In addition to making selections, the Selection tool can be used to change the shape of an object. You can click and drag the lines and corners to change an object's shape.

Changing an Object's Shape at the Corners

If you move the cursor over the corner of an object, it will change to ⬉. You can then drag to change the shape as shown below.

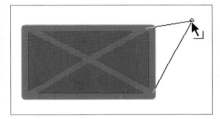

Changing an Object's Shape at a Line

When you place the mouse pointer over a line, the cursor will change to ⬎. This can be used to bend or add curves to the line.

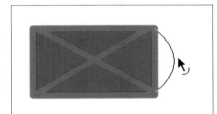

Using the Selection Tool to Copy Objects

The Selection tool can also create copies of an object. Select the object that is to be copied, hold down the Ctrl/Command or Alt/Option key, and drag the object to a new location. Your mouse pointer will display a plus sign and a copy of the original object will be created in the new location.

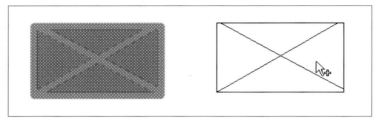

Using the Alt/Option key to copy an object

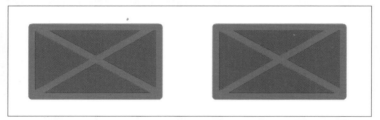

The duplicated object

Selecting Objects Using the Lasso Tool

To make irregularly shaped selections, press L on the keyboard to bring up the Lasso tool. You can then draw your selection on the Stage. Don't forget to close the selection!

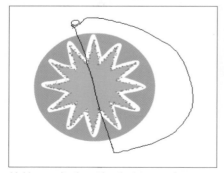

Making a selection using the Lasso tool

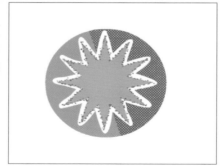

An area selected using the Lasso tool

Editing Bitmaps

The Lasso tool is especially useful for editing bitmap images because you can make detailed selections, as shown in the example below.

1. Select File > Import > Import to Stage to load a bitmap image into your movie.

2. Select Modify > Break apart from the menu or use the shortcut Ctrl-B (Command-B for Macintosh).

3. Use the Lasso tool to select the desired area within the image.

4. Remove the background and display only the selected image on the screen.

Lasso Tool Options

There are several options in the Toolbox that enable you to change how the Lasso tool works.

Magic Wand

The Magic Wand selects areas that are both adjacent to the point where you click and similar in color. This tool can be used in bitmap images to make a selection based on the colors in the image. You may want to hold down the Shift key to add to your original selection.

Magic Wand Settings

You can determine how closely the Magic Wand matches the clicked color by changing the Threshold value. Smoothing determines how smooth the selection's edges will be.

Ⓐ **Pixels**: The selection uses the rectangular edges of pixels.

Ⓑ **Rough**: An angular selection is created, with a harder edge than with the Pixels setting.

Ⓒ **Normal**: Selection is softer than the Pixels setting but rougher than the Smooth setting.

Ⓓ **Smooth**: Selection edges are rounded.

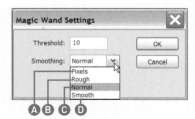

Polygon Mode

In Polygon mode, the Lasso tool creates polygonal or straight-line selections. Click the tool to mark the corners of the polygon, then double-click the last point to make the selection.

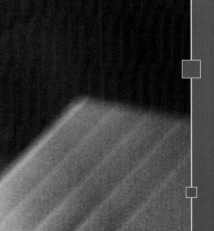

Advanced Drawing and Editing Tools

I n this section, we'll look at tools that allow for more advanced graphical techniques.

The Pen Tool and the Subselection Tool

The Pen (⬚) and Subselection tools (⬚) allow you to create complex objects. The Pen tool (⬚) creates a series of points that are joined by either straight or curved lines. The Subselection tool (⬚) enables you to select and work with the anchor points of objects drawn using the Line, Pencil, Oval, Rectangle, and Pen tools. Both of these tools take practice to master.

Using the Pen Tool to Draw Straight Lines

Select the Pen tool by pressing P on the keyboard. Choose the line color and thickness in the Properties panel and click in the Workspace to create the starting point for your line. Click again to create a second point, and a line will connect the two points.

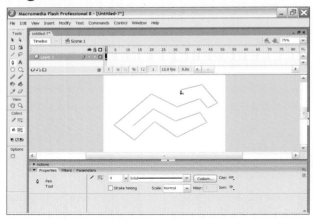

Drawing straight lines with the Pen tool

Using the Pen Tool to Draw Curves

Using the Pen tool to draw curves is a little more complicated than drawing straight lines. Choose the Pen tool, then click (and hold) the mouse button over the Workspace to create the starting point. Drag the mouse over the Workspace with the mouse button pressed to determine the direction and degree of your curve. Release the mouse button, then click and drag again to create a second point in your outline. The curve properties of this second point will be blended with those of the first to create a curved line between the two points. Continue to drag to add line segments to the drawing.

You will notice that handles appear as you create the curves. If you hold down the Shift key as you drag the Pen tool you will create only horizontal, vertical, and 45-degree handles.

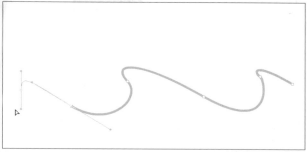

Drawing curves with the Pen tool

The Elements of a Bezier Curve

Curves drawn with the Pen tool are called Bezier curves and have anchor points and tangent handles.

- **Anchor Points**: Anchor points are created wherever the Pen tool is clicked. They represent the end of one section of the curve and the beginning of another.

- **Tangent Handles**: Tangent handles are the directional lines that appear at anchor points. You can drag the handles to adjust the curve.

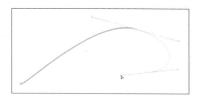

Using the Subselection Tool to Edit Objects

With the Subselection tool, you can manipulate the anchor points of objects drawn using the Line, Pencil, Oval, Rectangle, and Pen tools. Press A to bring up this tool.

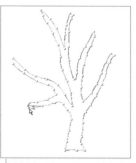

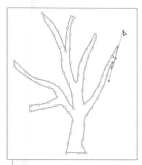

1 When you click on an object with the Subselection tool, the anchor points for the object will appear.

2 You can drag a point with the mouse to move it to a new location, or you can use the Left, Right, Up, and Down arrow keys on the keyboard to nudge it in the desired direction.

3 You can also drag the endpoints of the handles to change the shape of the curve. Both handles will move at the same time. If you want to adjust one of the handles, hold down the Alt/Option key while dragging.

The Free Transform tool enables you to change the skew, scale, rotation, and distortion of objects on the Stage. Press Q on the keyboard to use this tool.

There are four options for the Free Transform tool in the Options section of the Toolbox: Rotate and Skew (⬚), Scale (⬚), Distort (⬚), and Envelope (⬚).

To use the Free Transform tool, select an object on the stage and click the tool's button, then choose the type of transformation you want to apply from the Options section. You can also use the tool to click on the object that you want to transform. Once the Free Transform tool is applied to an object, it will show black handles that can be used for transformations.

Rotating an Object

You can use the standard Free Transform tool (▣) to rotate an object. Click outside one of the corners of the object, and the mouse cursor will change into a Rotate cursor (⟳). Drag the mouse to rotate the object.

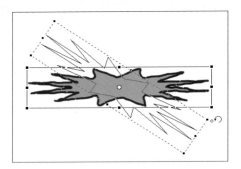

Skew Transform (⬚)

To use the Skew Transform, drag the center handle of a side to create a skewed effect.

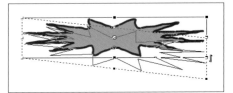

Scale Transform (⬚)

The Scale Transform is applied by selecting one of the black squares and dragging it to change the size of the object. If you drag a corner while holding down the Shift key, the object will retain its proportions.

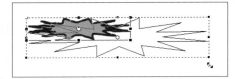

Distort Transform (⬚)

The Distort Transform allows you to drag each of the black squares independently of each other to distort the overall shape of the object.

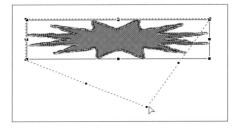

Hold down the Shift key while dragging to transform the object symmetrically.

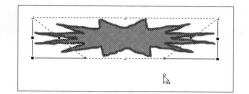

Envelope Transform ( )

The Envelope Transform uses both circular and rectangular handles to transform the shape. Circular handles contain tangent handles to create curves. Rectangular handles move the points as with a distortion transform.

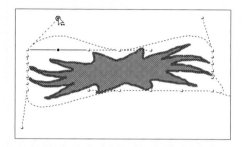

tip >>

Limits of Free Transform Options

Skew Transform ( ) and Scale Transform ( ) can be applied to all objects, but Distort Transform ( ) and Envelope Transform ( ) only work on shapes drawn with the Oval, Rectangle, Pencil, and Pen tools. Distort Transform and Envelope Transform can't be applied to grouped shapes or symbols.

The Transform Menu

Another way to transform a selected object on the Stage is to use the Modify > Transform menu selection.

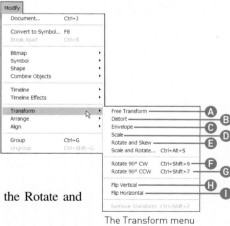

The Transform menu

A Free Transform: Activates the Free Transform tool.

B Distort: Activates the Free Transform tool with the Distort option selected in the Toolbox.

C Envelope: Activates the Free Transform tool with the Envelope option selected in the Toolbox.

D Scale: Activates the Free Transform tool with the Scale option selected in the Toolbox.

E Rotate and Skew: Activates the Free Transform tool with the Rotate and Skew option selected in the Toolbox.

F Rotate 90° CW: Rotates the selected object clockwise by 90 degrees.

G Rotate 90° CCW: Rotates the selected object counterclockwise by 90 degrees.

H Flip Vertical: Flips the selected object vertically (i.e., the top and bottom positions are reversed).

I Flip Horizontal: Flips the selected object horizontally (i.e., the left and right positions are reversed).

In this section, we'll look at tools that enable you to add color to objects.

The Paint Bucket Tool ()

The Paint Bucket tool fills an object with color. Press K on the keyboard to activate this tool.

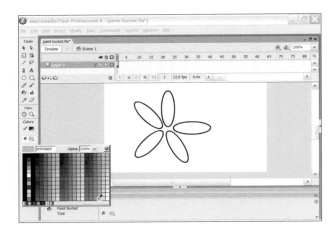

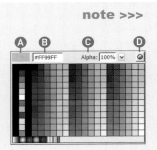

note >>>

Color Palette

- **A** **Color Preview**: Displays the selected color.
- **B** **Hexadecimal Text Box**: Displays the color value in the form of a hexadecimal number.
- **C** **Alpha**: Sets the alpha (transparency) of the color.
- **D** **System Color Picker**: Allows you to create custom colors.

Mixing and Saving Your Own Color

Instead of using the current swatches, you can mix your own color in the Color Palette.

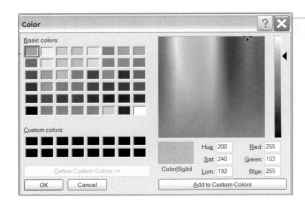

1 In the Color Palette, click on the System Color Picker button ( ).

2 The Color dialog box will appear. Select the color from the color space or enter the color values in the RGB (red, green, blue) or HSL (hue, saturation, luminosity) fields. If you want to save a new color, select a swatch under Custom Colors and click the Add to Custom Colors button.

tip >>

If the Paint Bucket tool can't fill your object, it's probably because you have gaps in the shape. The Paint Bucket tool works best with closed shapes. You can either fill in the gaps before using this tool or use the Options section of the Paint Bucket tool to change the Close Gaps setting.

Paint Bucket Tool Options

The options section of the Tools panel provides some different ways for the Paint Bucket tool to deal with gaps in the selected object.

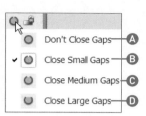

Ⓐ Don't Close Gaps: Colors only completely closed shapes.

Ⓑ Close Small Gaps: Colors shapes with very tiny gaps.

Ⓒ Close Medium Gaps: Colors shapes with medium-sized gaps.

Ⓓ Close Large Gaps: Colors shapes with large gaps. There is a limit to how large a gap Flash can deal with, so it is better to make the gaps as small as possible.

The Ink Bottle Tool (🖋)

The Ink Bottle tool is used to specify the color, thickness, and shape of lines. It can also be used to add a border to a borderless object. It is activated with the S key on the keyboard.

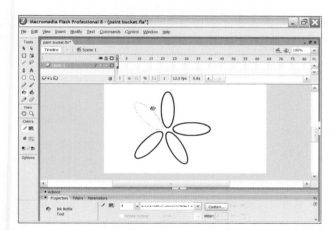

The Ink Bottle Tool Properties Panel

Ⓐ Stroke Color: Sets the color of the line.

Ⓑ Stroke Height: Sets the line thickness.

Ⓒ Stroke Style: Sets the line style.

Ⓓ Custom: The Custom button will open the Stroke Style dialog box, where you can create your own styles.

The Eyedropper Tool ( )

The Eyedropper tool samples color from an object on the Stage so you can apply the same color to another object. It can also sample from a bitmap image.

Sampling a color with the Eyedropper tool

After sampling a color, the Eyedropper tool changes to the Paint Bucket tool so you can fill a shape.

The Fill Transform Tool ( )

When an object has been filled with a gradient, the Fill Transform tool allows you to scale or rotate the gradient without changing the shape of the object. To activate the Fill Transform tool, press F on the keyboard.

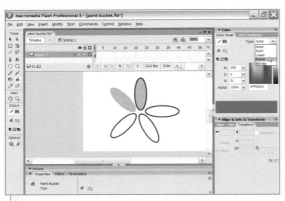

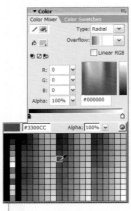

1 To create a gradient, select the type of gradient you want from the Color Mixer panel. You have a choice of Linear or Radial.

2 Double-click the existing pointers on the gradient bar and choose a color.

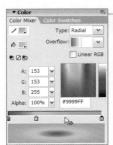

3 You can drag the pointers to a new location or add more pointers (up to 15) by clicking on the gradient bar. If necessary, you can remove pointers by dragging them out of the Color Mixer panel.

Applying and Transforming Gradients

Applying Radial Gradients

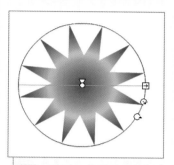

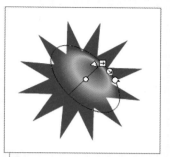

1 Apply a radial gradient by selecting the Color Mixer panel, choosing the Radial type setting, and selecting the colors. Draw a shape and it will be filled with the gradient. (You can also use the Paint Bucket tool to fill an existing shape.)

2 Click the gradient with the Fill Transform tool (▣) to activate five Fill Transform handles. The center circle handle allows you to change the location of the gradient within the shape, while the center triangle lets you change the focus. On the right, the top arrow handle changes the width of the fill while the middle handle increases and decreases the size of the fill. The bottom handle rotates the gradient.

Linear Gradients

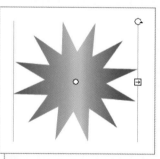

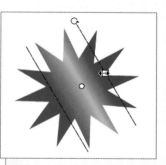

1 You can create a linear gradient by selecting the Linear option from the Color Mixer or by using the Paint Bucket tool.

2 Click the gradient with the Fill Transform tool to activate three Fill Transform handles. The center handle repositions the gradient, while the top handle rotates the fill. The remaining handle increases and decreases the width of the gradient.

Flash 8 includes a new feature for dealing with gradients that don't take up the entire area within a shape. The Overflow box allows you to choose from three options: no overflow (▣ ▾), reflection (▣▣▾), and repeat (▣▣▾) .

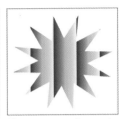

The no overflow option

The reflect overflow option

The repeat overflow option

Arranging Objects on the Stage

You can arrange objects on the stage using Modify > Arrange. The first four arrange options allow you to change the stacking order of objects that are located in the same place on the Stage. Using these options is a little like shuffling the order of a stack of cards to reveal some cards and hide others.

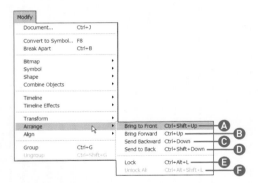

Ⓐ **Bring to Front**: Brings the selected object to the front of the Stage, on top of any other objects.

Ⓑ **Bring Forward**: Brings the selected object one "level" forward. If you repeat this option enough times, you'll eventually bring the selected object all the way to the front.

Ⓒ **Send Backward**: Moves the selected object one "level" backward. If you repeat this option enough times, you'll eventually send the selected object all the way to the back.

Ⓓ **Send to Back**: Moves the selected object to the bottom of all other objects.

Ⓔ **Lock**: Locks the selected object so that it cannot be selected.

Ⓕ **Unlock All**: Unlocks all locked objects.

Aligning Objects on the Stage

The Align panel allows you to arrange a group of objects on the Stage. You can bring up this panel by selecting Window > Design Panels > Align or with the shortcut Ctrl-K (Command-K on a Macintosh). The same options are also available in the Modify > Align menu.

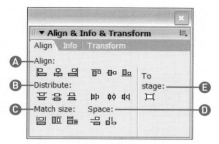

The Align tab in the Align & Info & Transform panel

Ⓐ Align: The first three buttons deal with left-to-right alignment:
- **Left align**: Aligns selected objects with the object farthest to the left.
- **Horizontal center alignment**: Aligns selected objects down the center.
- **Right align**: Aligns selected objects with the object farthest to the right.

The last three align buttons deal with top-to-bottom alignment:
- **Top align**: Aligns selected objects with the object closest to the top of the Stage.
- **Vertical center alignment**: Aligns selected objects halfway between the top and bottom of the Stage.
- **Bottom align**: Aligns selected objects with the object closest to the bottom of the Stage.

Ⓑ Distribute: The Distribute buttons on the second row control how the space between selected objects is distributed. From left to right, the buttons are top distribution, horizontal center distribution, bottom distribution, left distribution, vertical center distribution, and right distribution.

Ⓒ Match Size: The Match Size buttons allow you to change the size of the selected objects to the same height (vertical match), same width (horizontal match), or both (vertical and horizontal match).

Ⓓ Space: The two Space buttons allow you to space out selected objects evenly, either vertically or horizontally.

Ⓔ To stage: This button is used with the Distribute buttons. When it is checked, the selected objects are distributed according to the height or width of the Stage. Otherwise, distribution is calculated by the furthest positions of the selected objects.

Using the Trace Bitmap Command

Due to file size and Internet speed considerations, you will primarily work with vector images in Flash. Vector images are described by mathematical equations rather than pixel data, so they are considerably more efficient than bitmap images. Fortunately, Flash can convert bitmap images into vector shapes. This is useful for reducing file size, and it also allows you to work with Flash's vector-specific commands. You can bring up the Trace Bitmap dialog box by selecting Modify > Bitmap > Trace Bitmap. Note that tracing an image will usually reduce the quality of the original bitmap, and it can't recreate photorealistic images.

The Trace Bitmap Dialog Box

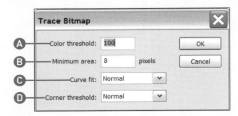

A **Color threshold**: This setting determines which color values are rounded off to the same color. The higher the value, the lower the number of different colors in the traced vector image.

B **Minimum area**: The minimum area indicates how many surrounding pixels will be averaged to determine a pixel's color. The higher the number, the fewer unique colors there will be in the vector image.

C **Curve fit**: This option lets you choose whether you want less detail and smoother lines in the vector image, or more detail with a corresponding increase in file size.

D **Corner threshold**: This option lets you choose fewer corners and a smaller file size, or more corners and a larger file size.

You will probably have to experiment with different settings before you are satisfied with the result. If you don't like what you get, press Ctrl-Z to undo (Command-Z on a Macintosh), then reapply the Trace Bitmap command with new settings.

Using Layers

If you have previously used graphics software packages, you will be familiar with the concept of layers. If you haven't, think of layers as pieces of transparent cellophane that are stacked on top of each other to create the final image. Putting different objects on different layers makes it easy for you to work with them separately. Layers appear on the left side of the Timeline.

Using Layer Folders

As you master more advanced Flash animation skills, the complexity of your work will grow. Eventually, you are likely to work on large projects, requiring the use of many layers. In this case, you can use layer folders to group similar layers together. When you right-click on a layer folder, its shortcut menu will pop up and you can choose to apply the same options to all the layers in the folder. The options available let you show, hide, lock, or unlock layers; you can also choose to show all layers in the folder as outlines.

- **Motion Guide Layer**: Using the Pen tool, you can draw the path along which your objects will move on the motion guide layer. Link the layer containing your objects to the motion guide layer to animate them along its path.

- **Mask Layer**: Mask layers filter the display of underlying graphic layers. Shapes drawn on a mask layer define the areas of the underlying graphic layer that are visible during movie playback. Areas lying outside the content of the mask layer are hidden.

- **Current Layer**: The current layer is the active layer on which you can draw or add objects. In the Timeline, you will see a pencil icon next to the current layer.

- **Show/Hide All Layers**: Use this to display or hide the items on all the layers.

- **Lock/Unlock All Layers**: Use this to lock or unlock all the layers.

- **Show All Layers as Outlines**: This icon allows you to view all of the layers in outlines. This menu contains submenus that you can use to customize the outline view.

Inserting Layers

By default, when you open a new document in Flash, it will contain a single frame on a single layer. You can add layers by selecting a layer and clicking on the Add Layer icon (⊞) in the Timeline. You can also add layers by choosing Insert > Layer from the menu bar, or by right-clicking on a layer and selecting Insert Layer from the shortcut menu that appears. New layers are always added above the currently selected layer. You can change the name of a layer by double-clicking on its name and typing in the new name.

Moving Layers

Layers are stacked one on top of another in a certain order. To change a layer's place in the order, simply drag the layer to its desired position in the Timeline.

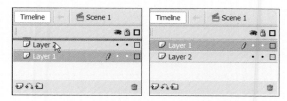

Deleting Layers

To delete a layer, select it in the Timeline and click on the Delete Layer icon (🗑). Another way of deleting a layer is to right-click it and select Delete Layer from the shortcut menu. To delete several layers at once, click the layers you wish to delete one at a time while holding down the Ctrl/Command key, then click on the Delete Layer icon (🗑).

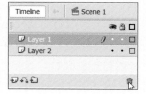

1   Creating a Logo with Text

Flash 8 makes creating special effects with text much easier than in previous versions. In this section, we'll use the Text tool with the Transform tool to create a logo with text.

Start File
   02_001.fla

Final File
   02_001_end.fla

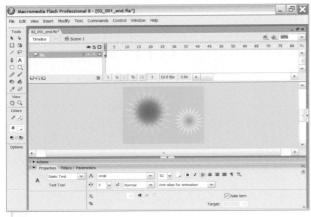

[1] Open the start file and click the Insert Layer button to add a new layer. Name it "text" and select frame 1 in the new layer.

[2] Select the Text tool and, in the Properties panel, change the font to Arial, the size to 52 pt, and the text (fill) color to White. Click the Bold button.

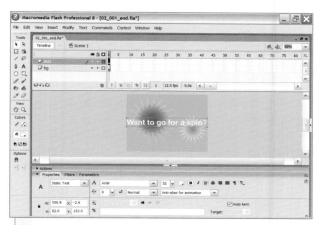

3 Click in the middle of the Stage and enter "Want to go for a spin?"

4 Click the Selection tool. The text appears in a text field surrounded by a blue box. Because the text is grouped, anything we do will affect all letters.

5 Right-click the text and select Break Apart from the shortcut menu. You can also use the Ctrl-B shortcut (Command-B on a Macintosh).

6 The text is broken down into individual letters.

7 Apply Break Apart again to create a shape from each letter.

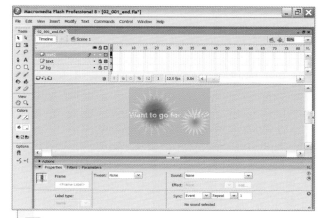

8 With the letter shapes still selected, copy them using Edit > Copy and create a new layer. Name the new layer "text2" and lock the bg and text layers by clicking the Lock icon ( ). Choose Edit > Paste in Place to position the copied text in the same location as the original.

9 Click in the grey pasteboard to deselect the text. Select the Ink Bottle tool and set the stroke color to #CC66CC. Choose a solid line with a size of 2.

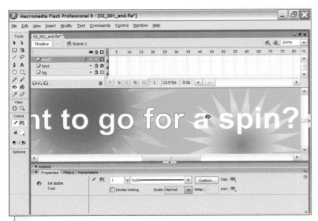

10 Click on the edge of each letter to add a border. You should probably zoom into the image first. It may be necessary to click both the inside and outside edges for the letters o, g, and a.

11 Select the bg layer and click on the Add Layer icon to add a new layer. Name the layer "text3". Hold down the Alt/Option key and drag the frame from the text2 layer into the new layer. This creates a copy. Lock the text2 layer.

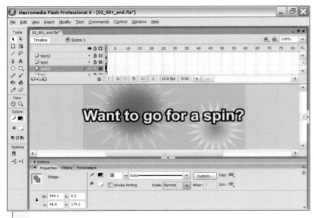

12 Use the Selection tool to drag a selection box around the text, and change the stroke color to black and the size to 10 pt in the Properties panel.

13 Unlock all the locked layers except the bg layer by clicking each of the Lock icons.

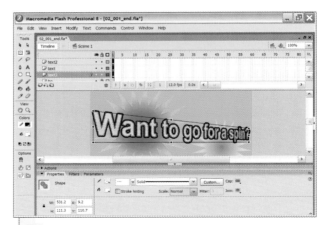

14 Use the Selection tool to drag a selection box around the text. This will select the text on all layers.

15 Choose the Free Transform tool (⊞) and select the Distort option (▱). Use the tool to distort each corner of the text as shown here. Make sure the "Want" side is higher than the "spin" side.

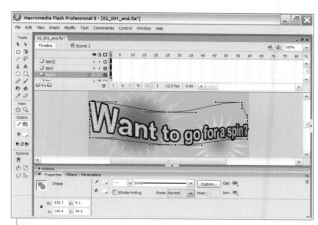

16 Select the Envelope option () to transform the text even more. As shown, move the center point down and adjust the handles at each point to create a curved shape.

17 Click the Selection tool to deselect the text and test the movie using the Ctrl-Enter shortcut (Command-Return on a Macintosh).

tip >>

Undoing

Using Shortcut Keys

If you've made a mistake and want to undo the last step, you can use the shortcut Ctrl-Z (Command-Z on a Macintosh). Repeat this shortcut to undo more than one step.

Using Menus

You can also undo the last step by choosing Edit > Undo from the menu bar.

Using the History Panel

The History panel contains a list of all the actions you've carried out in the current movie. You can click on a step in the panel to return to that point.

2 Drawing a Rabbit

Drawing images in Flash requires a lot of practice. In this example, we'll draw a rabbit to help you become more familiar with Flash's drawing tools. We'll also explore some options that allow you to change the arrangement, position, and alignment of an object.

Start File
02_002.fla

Final File
02_002_end.fla

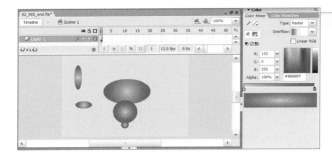

1 Open the start file. Open the Color Mixer panel and choose a radial gradient as the fill style. Select a dark purple color for the right end of the gradient and a lighter purple for the left end.

2 Select frame 1 of Layer 1 and choose the Oval tool ( ). Choose no stroke color and click the Object Drawing button ( ) in the Options section of the Tools panel. Draw the oval shapes as shown.

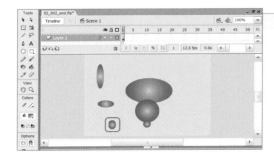

3 Double-click the Rectangle tool. In the Rectangle Settings dialog box, set the Corner Radius to 20 points and click OK.

4 Use the Rectangle tool to draw a foot shape at the bottom as shown.

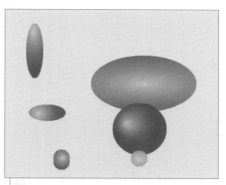

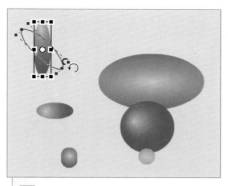

5 Use the Fill Transform tool to adjust the gradients as shown.

6 Rotate the ear shape about 45° using the Free Transform tool.

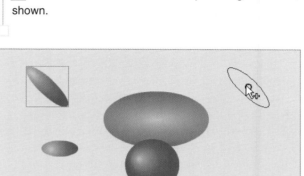

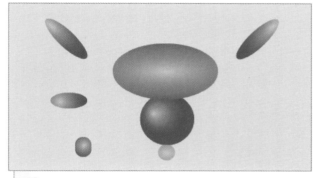

7 Select the ear shape with the Selection tool. Hold down the Alt/Option and Shift keys and drag it to the opposite side of the Stage to create a copy.

8 To make the copy a mirror image of the first ear, select Modify > Transform > Flip Horizontal from the menu bar.

9 Select the middle of the three center shapes and choose Modify > Arrange > Send to Back to place it behind the head shape. Move the bottom circle so that it just touches the middle circle.

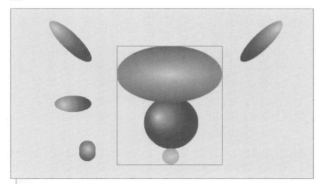

10 Select the head, body, and tail shapes by holding down the Shift key as you click them, then use the Ctrl-G shortcut to group them together (Command-G on a Macintosh).

11 Place the two ears on either side of the head, making sure they're behind as shown.

12 Slightly rotate the arm and foot. Repeat steps 7 and 8 to duplicate the arm and foot. Place them on the body as shown. Make sure you position the arms behind the body and the feet in front of the body.

13 Add a new layer to the Timeline. Rename Layer 1 to "body" and lock it. Rename Layer 2 to "face."

14 Choose the Oval tool and select black as the fill color. Draw two circles for eyes.

15 Change the fill color to white and draw two more circles for the whites of the eyes.

16 User the Line tool to draw whiskers as shown. Use a stroke height of 2 and a black color.

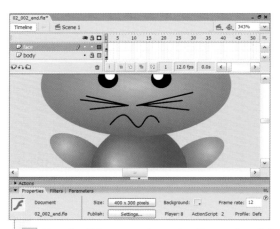

17 Use the P key to activate the Pen tool and draw the mouth as shown.

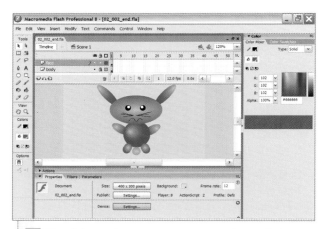

18 The finished image is shown here. Press Ctrl-Enter (Command-Return on a Macintosh) to test the movie.

3

Adding Scrolling Text to Flash Movies

Flash movies often use scrolling text, which you can easily create by adding a TextArea component to the Stage.

Start File
02_003.fla

Final File
02_003_end.fla

1 Open the start file and bring up the Components panel with the Ctrl-F7 shortcut (Command-F7 on a Macintosh). Scroll down in the User Interface category until you can see the TextArea component.

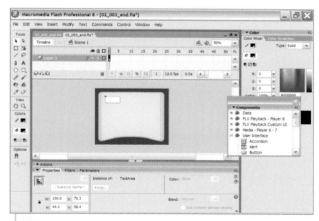

2 Drag a component onto the Stage and position it as shown.

tip >>

What Is a Component?

A component is a special movie clip that is provided with Flash. Flash 8 includes many components such as checkboxes and push-buttons. Programmers can also build their own components.

3 In the Properties panel, increase the size of the component by entering the following settings: W: 350, H: 150, X: 70, Y: 60.

4 Switch to the Parameters tab in the Properties panel and click the space to the right of the word "text." Enter the following text: "Here is some text in a TextArea component." (You could enter more text if you wanted. You could also change the html setting to "true" and enter basic HTML tags in the text.)

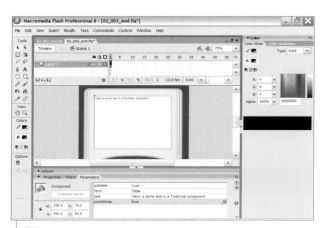

5 The Stage should look as shown here.

6 Test the movie using the Ctrl-Enter shortcut (Command-Return on a Macintosh). Add more text to the TextArea component until you see the scrollbar appear on the right. Note that you can use the cut, copy, and paste commands with this component.

tip >>

Advanced TextArea Option

Programmers can load text into the TextArea component from a file outside of Flash. They can also save the text that a user enters into a component.

4

Working with Bitmap Images

Although Flash 8 is designed primarily for use with vector images, it can also work with bitmap images such as JPEG, PNG, and GIF files. You can convert a bitmap image into a vector image by using Flash's Trace Bitmap command. You can also break a bitmap into blocks of color and use it as a fill for shapes. In this exercise, you will use a bitmap image to fill a shape.

Import File
sunset.jpg

Final File
02_004_end.fla

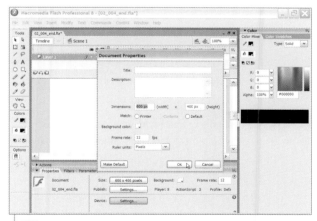

1 Select File > New from the menu bar or Create New > Flash Document from the Start Page. In the Properties panel, change the document size to 600 × 400 pixels.

2 Select File > Import > Import to Stage and choose the file sunset.jpg. Click Open.

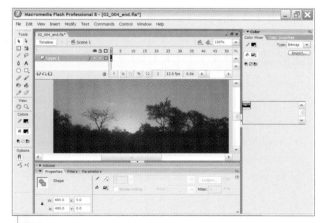

3 Use the Ctrl-B shortcut (Command-B on a Macintosh) to break apart the image. This converts the image into blocks of color that can be selected with the Eyedropper tool.

71

4 Use the Eyedropper tool to sample the image. This will allow you to use the bitmap as a fill for any shapes you add to the stage.

5 Delete the image using the Delete key and double-click the Rectangle tool to bring up the Rectangle Settings dialog box. Change the Corner Radius value to 10 and click OK.

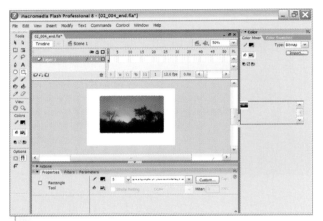

6 In the Properties panel, set the stroke style to a speckled line, the color to black, and the height to 5. In the Color Mixer panel, change the fill type to Bitmap.

7 Draw a rectangle on the Stage as shown here. It should be filled with the sampled bitmap image.

8 Press Ctrl-Enter (Command-Return on a Macintosh) to test the movie.

tip >>

The Import Command

Flash's Import command allows you import files including bitmap images, sound files, video files, Illustrator files, and other Flash .swf files. The import options will change depending on the type of file you have chosen.

To import files onto the Stage, either select File > Import > Import to Stage from the menu bar or use the shortcut Ctrl-R (Command-R on a Macintosh). When the Import dialog box appears, select the file to be imported and press the Open button. We will cover importing sound and video files in more detail later in the book.

Let`s Go Pro!

Drawing Models in Flash

Flash 8 offers two different ways to draw shapes: the Merge Drawing model and the Object Drawing model. Merge Drawing has been available in all previous versions of Flash, while the Object Drawing model is new to Flash 8.

In this chapter, we've focused mainly on the Merge Drawing model. Using this method, where you draw overlapping objects on the same layer, the top object will affect the one underneath when you separate them. Objects drawn with this method are referred to as "shapes."

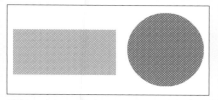

Objects drawn with the Merge Drawing model show dots when selected.

When you separate overlapping objects, the top shape affects the shape underneath.

The only way to avoid this effect when using Merge Drawing is to draw each object on a separate layer.

Flash 8 offers the Object Drawing model when you use the Pencil, Line, Pen, Brush, Oval, Rectangle, and Polygon tools. Select one of these tools and you'll see the Object Drawing button (▣) in the Options section of the Tools panel. To use the Object Drawing model, you need to click the button before you draw your objects.

When you use the Object Drawing model, objects that overlap won't affect each other. You can overlap and separate them as necessary. When you use this drawing model, you create "drawing objects" rather than shapes.

Objects drawn with the Object Drawing model show a blue box when selected.

tip >>

You can change from one drawing model to another after you've drawn your objects. To go from the Merge Drawing to the Object Drawing model, select one or more shapes and choose Modify > Combine Objects > Union from the menu bar. To go from a drawing objects to drawing shapes, use Modify > Break Apart or the Ctrl-B shortcut (Command-B on a Macintosh).

Import File
elly.ai

Inserting Illustrator Files

Adobe Illustrator is a popular, vector-based graphics program that you can use to draw images that are difficult to draw with Flash alone. Like Illustrator, Flash uses layers; this makes it possible for work done with layers to be shared across programs. Flash files that are exported to Illustrator retain all of their layer properties such as layer name, lock/unlock/hide/show status, and so on. When exporting Illustrator files to Flash, you should first save them as an Illustrator 10.0 or earlier file.

01 Create a new Flash file by choosing File > New and selecting Flash Document.

02 We'll now import an Illustrator file into Flash, preserving the layers. Select File > Import > Import to Stage from the menu bar. The Import command is used to place other types of files into Flash. External files that are imported into Flash appear as objects.

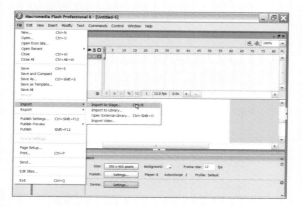

03 In the Import dialog box, select elly.ai from the Sample folder and click Open.

04 This will open the Illustrator Import dialog box. In the Convert area, make sure that Layers is chosen and click OK.

05 As you can see from the Timeline, the layers are imported into Flash with the same properties and stacking order as they had in the Illustrator document.

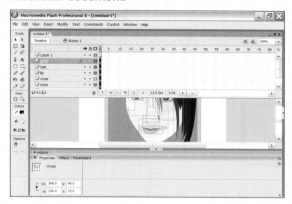

note >>>

The Illustrator Import Dialog Box

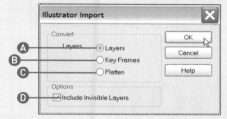

Ⓐ Layers: Converts the layers in the Illustrator document into layers in the Flash document.

Ⓑ Keyframes: The layers are imported into Flash as keyframes in the order they were stacked in Illustrator. The layer name becomes the frame label.

Ⓒ Flatten: All the layers in the Illustrator document are combined into one layer in the Flash document.

Ⓓ Include Invisible Layers: Any layers that are hidden in the Illustrator document are also imported into Flash. (Normally, these layers would be excluded from the import.)

Chapter | 3

Basic Elements of Animation

Flash animations are created by playing a series of static images to give the effect of movement. This is the same effect that is created when you flip through a book with sequential drawings on each page. In this chapter, we will spend some time learning about the basic structure and elements of Flash animations. These will include the Timeline, Timeline effects, symbols, and the Library.

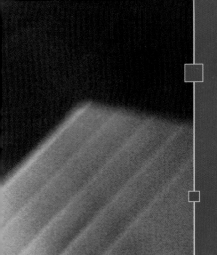

Understanding the Basic Elements

The Timeline, located just above the Stage, is the primary tool with which you control animations in Flash. Since the idea behind the Timeline is so important to animating in Flash, we will spend some time looking at the structure and elements of the Timeline to make sure that you fully grasp the concepts before moving on.

The Structure of the Timeline

Since you'll do most of your work in the Timeline, use the following section to familiarize yourself with how it works.

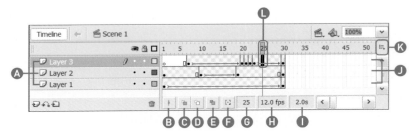

Ⓐ Layers: As discussed in Chapter 2, you can think of layers as transparent sheets stacked on top of one another. In addition to the normal layers, you can insert motion guide layers, layer folders, and mask layers. To keep the layers organized and easy to identify, give them descriptive names.

Ⓑ Center Frame button: Moves the frame marked by the Playhead to the center of the Timeline.

Ⓒ Onion Skin button: When this button is pressed, a Start Onion Skin marker and an End Onion Skin marker will appear around the Playhead on the Timeline. This function lets you view a few frames before and after the current frame. Only the contents of the current frame will appear as normal; the rest will look semi-transparent. Additionally, only the current frame can be edited.

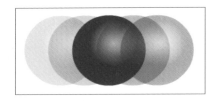

Ⓓ Onion Skin Outlines button: This is the same as the Onion Skin command, except that all frames but the current frame are displayed as outlines.

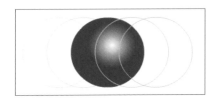

Ⓔ Edit Multiple Frames button: When you use the Onion Skin feature, you can only select the object in the current frame. Turning on the Edit Multiple Frames feature, however, allows you to edit objects in other frames at the same time.

F Modifying Onion Markers button: The following dropdown menu appears when this button is clicked.

- **Always Show Markers**: Always displays the Onion Skin markers on the Timeline, regardless of whether Onion Skin is turned on or off.

- **Anchor Onion Markers**: Locks the markers to their current positions on the Timeline so that they will not move with the Playhead.

- **Onion 2**: Shows two frames on either side of the current frame.

- **Onion 5**: Shows five frames on either side of the current frame.

- **Onion All**: Shows all frames.

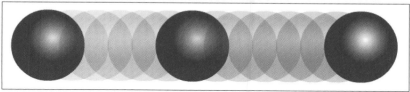

The Onion All setting

G Current Frame indicator: Shows the frame currently displayed on the Stage.

H Frame Rate indicator: This is the speed at which the animation is played, measured in frames per second (fps). Double-clicking it opens the Document Properties dialog box, where you can change the frame rate.

I Elapsed Time indicator: Displays how long the animation has been playing, in seconds.

J Frame: The frames in a layer are shown to the right of the layer name. Each frame contains a still image, and as these images are shown in sequence, the illusion of movement is created.

K Frames View pop-up menu: You can change the way frames are displayed in the Timeline by selecting options from the Frame View pop-up menu.

- **Tiny, Small, Normal, Medium, Large**: These are frame display size options.

- **Preview**: Shows a thumbnail of the objects in each frame (see below).

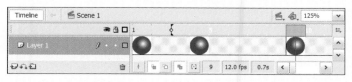

- **Preview in Context**: Shows a thumbnail of the entire frame, including white space, so you can see how the object changes position in the animation (see below).

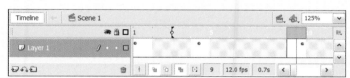

- **Short**: Shortens the height of frames. When you have many layers, this option makes it possible for you to see more layers in the Timeline.

- **Tinted Frames**: Displays the frame sequences with different tints. The tint will not show up on the Stage; it is only used to differentiate the frames in the Timeline.

🄛 **The Playhead**: The Playhead indicates the current frame that is being displayed on the Stage. To display a particular frame on the Stage, you can click and drag the Playhead along the Timeline.

tip >>

Frames and Keyframes

There are two types of frames in Flash: frames and keyframes. When you add content to a frame, you will automatically turn it into a keyframe. Keyframes can be edited and are marked on the Timeline with a solid black circle. Frames cannot be edited. Frames are either empty or, if they are between two keyframes, contain content interpolated from the keyframes on either side. The interpolated content creates the animation steps between the keyframes. In other words, frames only offer a preview of animation and as such, can't be edited. Keyframes that do not contain any content are called empty keyframes and are indicated by an empty circle.

When you open a new document, you will see a single layer containing a frame (marked with a circle) in the Timeline. To the right of this frame are dimmed cells. To use a cell, you have to turn it into a frame, a keyframe, or an empty keyframe.

Adding Frames or Keyframes

First, select the cell where you want to insert a frame. Then choose Insert > Timeline > Blank Keyframe or Insert > Timeline > Keyframe from the menu bar. Another way to insert frames or keyframes is to right-click on the cell or frame and choose Insert Frame or Insert Keyframe from the shortcut menu when it appears.

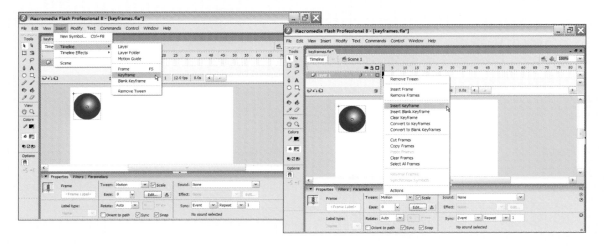

Removing Frames and Clearing Keyframes

When a frame is removed, the entire frame is deleted, reducing the total number of frames you have in the Timeline. On the other hand, when you clear a keyframe, you only remove the keyframe property and return the frame back to normal. The total number of frames in the Timeline will remain unchanged.

To delete or clear a frame, choose Edit > Timeline > Remove Frames or Edit > Timeline > Clear Frames. You can also right-click on a cell and choose either Remove Frames or Clear Frames.

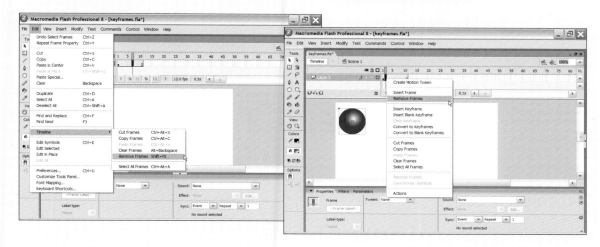

Moving Frames and Keyframes

To move a frame in the Timeline, click on the frame or keyframe that you wish to move and drag it to a new location.

Copying Frames and Keyframes

If you hold down the Alt/Option key while dragging a frame or keyframe to a new location, you will create a copy. Alternatively, you can click on the frame you want to copy and choose Edit > Timeline > Copy Frames from the menu bar, then click on the new location and choose Edit > Timeline > Paste Frames to make a copy.

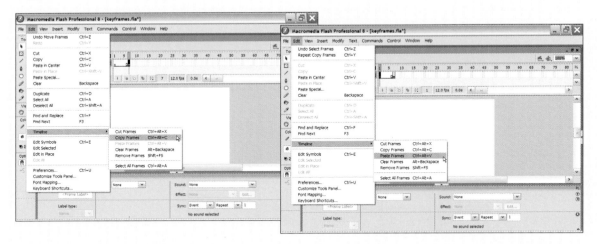

Shortcut Menus and Shortcut Keys for Frames

You can right-click on any frame to open the shortcut menu for that particular frame. The menu contains commands that can be applied to the selected frame. To work fast, it is a good idea to memorize the shortcut keys for these commands. Note that Macintosh users should substitute the Option key for the Alt key.

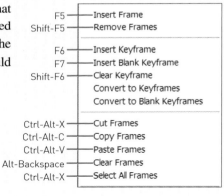

82

Working with Symbols and Libraries

Symbols are special objects that you can create in Flash, and they provide an advantage when it comes to reducing the size of your Flash movies. Normally, Flash stores every object in your animation separately, even if the same objects are used repeatedly, so each object contributes to your final file size. By converting objects into symbols, you allow Flash to store a single "master" object that can be used repeatedly without increasing your file size. Any time you use an object more than once, you should be working with symbols.

You can turn an existing object into a symbol, or you can create a new empty symbol that you can draw from scratch. It is normally easier to create a symbol from an existing object. All symbols for the movie are stored in the Library so they can be dragged onto the Stage when needed. Dragging a copy of a symbol to the Stage is called "creating an instance" of the symbol. You can change the properties of an instance—such as color, size, and position—without affecting the Library copy, but when you update the Library copy, all instances on the Stage change.

Types of Symbols

Flash works with three types of symbols: graphics, buttons, and movie clips. In this section, we will learn how to work with graphic and button symbols. We will also learn a little about the Library.

Graphic Symbols

Graphic symbols are used as images within a movie. These are images that you want to use more than once. Graphic symbols are often used in simple animations.

Button Symbols

Button symbols are symbols that react to the mouse, and they are often used to make menus and navigation systems. Button symbols have their own Timeline that looks different from the main Timeline. Instead of numbered frames, the Timeline for button symbols contains four frames: Up, Over, Down, and Hit.

- **Up**: The normal appearance of the button when there is no mouse interaction with the button.
- **Over**: The appearance when the mouse moves over or rests on the button.
- **Down**: The appearance when the user clicks or holds down the mouse button over the button.
- **Hit**: This frame shows which part of the button is clickable.

Movie Clip Symbols

A movie clip is a symbol with its own Timeline. It allows you to create an animation that is independent of anything happening on the main Timeline.

Creating a New Symbol

To create a new symbol, choose Insert > New Symbol from the menu bar or use the shortcut Ctrl-F8 (Command-F8 on a Macintosh). In the Create New Symbol dialog box, give the symbol a name, select a symbol type, and click OK.

Converting an Existing Object to a Symbol

The Convert to Symbol dialog box is used to create a symbol from an existing object. Open this dialog box by choosing Modify > Convert to Symbol or by using the shortcut key F8. You can enter the following information:

A **Name**: The name is used to reference the symbol in the Library. It is important to select a meaningful name so that you can find your symbol easily.

B **Type**: Selects the type of symbol to create.

C **Registration**: The registration point is used by Flash when symbols are positioned and transformed during an animation. The animation effects can change significantly depending on where the registration point is located within a symbol.

D **Advanced**: The Advanced button reveals additional options at the bottom of the dialog box. These options are usually used by programmers when ActionScripting. When the Advanced section is open, the button text changes to Basic.

Editing a Symbol

Editing a symbol is useful if you need to modify the symbol's appearance. You will also need to edit blank symbols to add content to them. When you edit a symbol, any copies or instances that are on the Stage will also change.

To edit a symbol, right-click it and select Edit from the shortcut menu that appears. You can also edit the symbol from the Library. Choose Window > Library, right-click the symbol name, and choose Edit. The symbol will then appear in editing mode. You will notice that the Timeline title includes the name of the symbol being edited, and that you are no longer working on the Stage.

You can make changes to your symbol using the drawing tools. When you have finished, click Scene 1 at the top of the Timeline to return to the Stage. Any instances of the symbol should reflect the changes you made.

Symbol Instance Properties

Each time you add a symbol instance to the Stage, you can change properties such as brightness, tint, and alpha. These options can be found in the Color drop-down box of the Properties panel when an instance is selected.

Brightness deals with the amount of white or black in an instance. It is a little like camera exposure. A normal instance has a Brightness value of 0%. As you increase the value towards 100% the instance becomes whiter and whiter. It will be completely white at a setting of 100%. Reducing Brightness below 0% adds black to the image, until it is totally black at -100%.

Tint adds a color on top of the existing instance. To use this setting, you must first select a color and then choose the tint percentage. A Tint value of 100% will completely fill the instance with the new color. Lesser values will provide a shading effect.

The alpha property deals with the transparency of the instance. A value of 100% means that the instance is totally visible. Values less than 100% fade the instance until at 0%, the instance is no longer visible. The alpha property is often used for fade-in and fade-out effects in an animation.

The Library

The Library contains all of the symbols that have been created in a movie; each type of symbol has a different icon. The Library may also contain sounds, video, components, and bitmap graphics. You can view the Library by using the Ctrl-L shortcut (Command-L on a Macintosh) or by choosing Window > Library.

You can add a symbol to the Stage by dragging it from the Library window. You can also organize your Library contents into folders.

Understanding Movie Clip Symbols

Sample File
- 03_001.fla

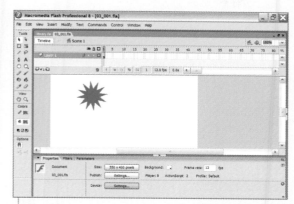

1 When you open the sample file, you will see a simple star symbol on the Stage.

2 Press Ctrl-Enter (Command-Return for Macintosh) to test the movie. Even though the movie clip only takes up one frame in the main Timeline, the star will appear to be rotating. This is because the movie clip has its own Timeline with more than one frame.

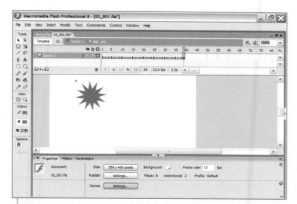

3 Close the test movie and double-click the star shape to edit the symbol in place. If you look at the Timeline, you'll see that the movie clip has its own 39-frame animation. This animation is completely independent of the main Timeline.

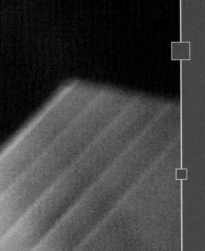

Understanding Timeline Effects

Timeline Effects allow you to create simple animations with a single mouse click. Normally, the process of creating animations involves working with objects over many frames and layers. However, this has been greatly simplified with Timeline Effects. Creating an animation can be as simple as entering settings into a Timeline Effects dialog box.

In this section, we'll summarize the Timeline Effects available in Flash 8 and look at the options that you can change.

Basic Effects

The basic Timeline Effects in Flash 8 include Copy to Grid, Distributed Duplicate, Blur, Drop Shadow, Expand, and Explode.

The Copy to Grid Effect

Copy to Grid duplicates and arranges an object on the Stage. You can apply this effect by choosing Insert > Timeline Effects > Assistants > Copy to Grid from the menu bar.

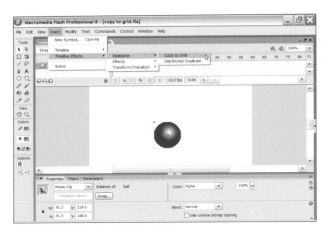 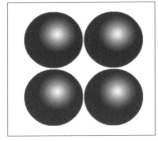

The Copy to Grid Dialog Box

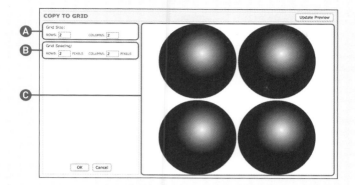

Ⓐ Grid Size:
- **Rows**: The number of rows of shapes to display.
- **Columns**: The number of columns of shapes to display.

Ⓑ Grid Spacing:
- **Rows**: The distance between rows in pixels.
- **Columns**: The distance between columns in pixels.

Ⓒ Update Preview: Each time you change the Timeline Effect settings, you will need to click the Update Preview button to see the effect.

The Distributed Duplicate Effect

The Distributed Duplicate effect allows you to create and modify duplicates of your shape on the Stage. You can apply it by choosing Insert > Timeline Effects > Assistants > Distributed Duplicate from the menu bar.

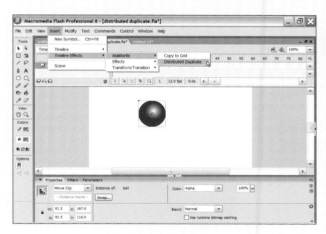

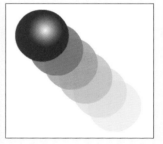

The Distributed Duplicate Dialog Box

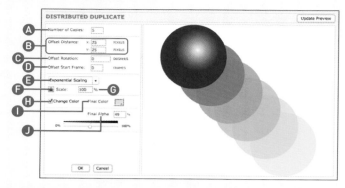

ⓐ Number of Copies: The number of copies to create.

ⓑ Offset Distance:
- **X**: The distance between copies, from left to right, in pixels.
- **Y**: The distance between copies, from top to bottom, in pixels.

ⓒ Offset Rotation: The number of degrees to rotate each copy.

ⓓ Offset Start Frame: The number of frames before the appearance of each copy.

ⓔ Exponential/Linear Scaling: Applies the scaling percentage linearly (constant change) or exponentially (increasing rate of change).

ⓕ Lock/Unlock: Activate lock to scale the width and height using the same percentage value. Unlock to apply different percentage values to width and height.

ⓖ Scale: Change the size of the duplicates by the indicated percentage.

ⓗ Change Color: Check this box to include a color change with copies.

ⓘ Final Color: The color of the last copy.

ⓙ Final Alpha: The transparency of the final copy, expressed as a percentage.

The Blur Effect

The Blur effect creates and animates semi-transparent copies of an object to give the effect of a motion blur. You can add this effect by selecting an object and choosing Insert > Timeline Effects > Effects > Blur. You can also right-click an object and choose Timeline Effects from the shortcut menu.

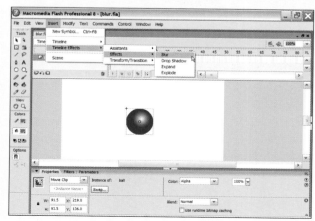

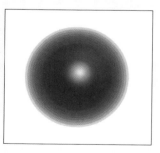

The Blur Dialog Box

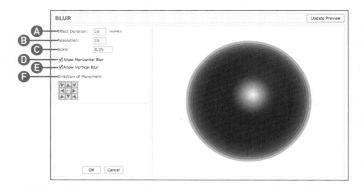

Ⓐ **Effect Duration**: The duration of the effect in frames. The higher this number, the longer the animation will take to complete.

Ⓑ **Resolution**: The total number of blurred objects.

Ⓒ **Scale**: The width of the blurred objects. The lower the number, the wider the visible border of the blurred objects.

Ⓓ **Allow Horizontal Blur**: The blur effect is applied horizontally.

Ⓔ **Allow Vertical Blur**: The blur effect is applied vertically.

Ⓕ **Direction of Movement**: The direction in which the animation will move. Selecting the center option distributes the effect evenly among the selected shapes.

The Drop Shadow Effect

The Drop Shadow effect applies a shadow to the selected object. Choose Insert > Timeline Effects > Effects > Drop Shadow from the menu bar.

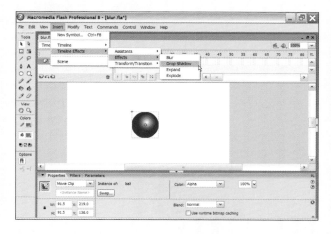

The Drop Shadow Dialog Box

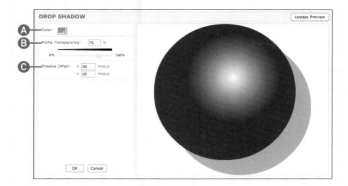

Ⓐ **Color**: The color of the shadow.

Ⓑ **Alpha Transparency**: The transparency of the shadow as a percentage.

Ⓒ **Shadow Offset**: The distance of the shadow from the shape in pixels.

The Expand Effect

This effect contracts and expands an object over a specified number of frames. You can apply this effect by choosing Insert > Timeline Effects > Effects > Expand from the menu bar.

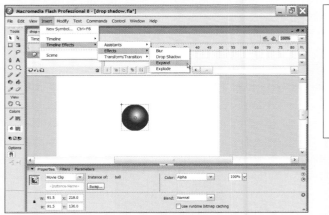

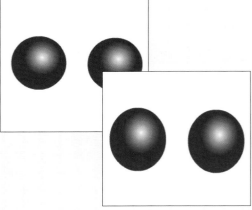

The Expand Dialog Box

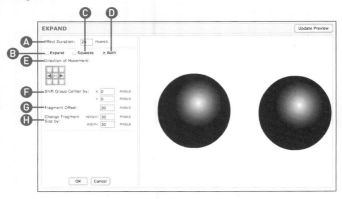

Ⓐ **Expand duration**: The duration of the effect in frames.

Ⓑ **Expand**: Animation expands the object.

Ⓒ **Squeeze**: Animation squeezes the object.

Ⓓ **Both**: Animation expands then squeezes the object.

Ⓔ **Direction of Movement**: The direction in which the animation moves.

Ⓕ **Shift Group Center by**: The distance in pixels that the center of the group is moved.

Ⓖ **Fragment Offset**: The space between elements.

Ⓗ **Change Fragment Size by**: The change in size of each fragment in pixels.

The Explode Effect

The Explode Timeline Effect creates an animation in which the object seems to explode on the Stage. Choose Insert > Timeline Effects > Effects > Explode from the menu bar.

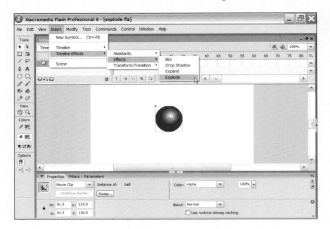
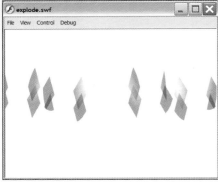

The Explode Dialog Box

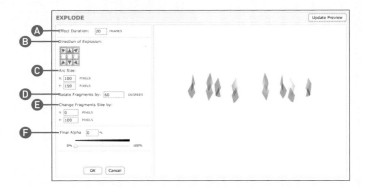

Ⓐ **Effect Duration**: The duration of the effect in frames.

Ⓑ **Direction of Explosion**: The direction in which the pieces are thrown during the explosion.

Ⓒ **Arc Size**: The distance that the exploded pieces are thrown in pixels.

Ⓓ **Rotate Fragments by**: The rotation of fragments during the explosion, in degrees.

Ⓔ Change Fragments Size by: The change in size of fragments during the explosion, in pixels.

Ⓕ Final Alpha: The final transparency setting, expressed as a percentage.

Transform and Transition Effects

Flash also offers Timeline Effects that allow you to create transformations and transitions.

The Transform Effect

The Transform effect can be used to apply movement and scaling animations to shapes. You can select it by choosing Insert > Timeline Effects > Transform/Transition > Transform from the menu bar.

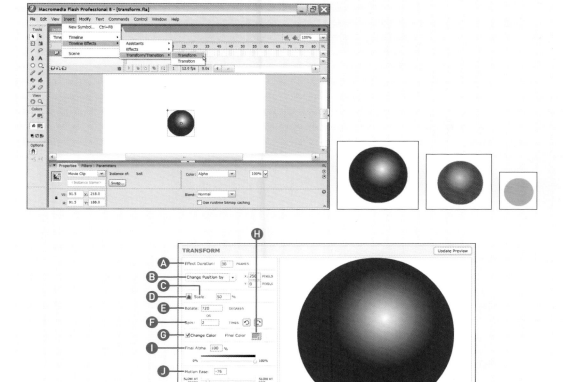

Ⓐ Effect Duration: The duration of the effect in frames.

Ⓑ Change Position by: The movement of the object during the animation, given as X and Y pixel values.

Ⓒ Scale: Changes the size of the shape by the given percentage.

Ⓓ Lock/Unlock: Activate lock to scale the width and height using the same percentage value. Unlock to apply different percentage values to width and height.

Ⓔ Rotate: Rotation during the effect, in degrees.

F **Spin**: Number of spins during the effect. Select clockwise or counterclockwise.

G **Change Color**: Check this option to include a color change.

H **Final Color**: If a color change is included, determines the color at the end of the animation.

I **Final Alpha**: The final transparency, expressed as a percentage.

J **Motion Ease**: Determines whether the animation accelerates or decelerates.

The Transition Effect

The Transition effect can be used to animate an object's entrance to or exit from the Stage using wiping and fading effects. Choose Insert > Timeline Effects > Transform/Transition > Transition from the menu bar.

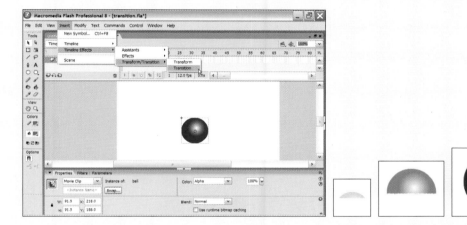

The Transition Dialog Box

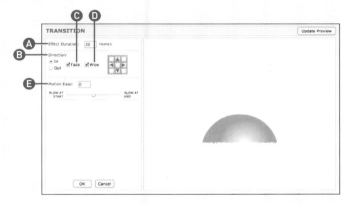

A **Effect Duration**: The duration of the effect in frames.

B **Direction**: The In setting makes shapes appear during the animation; the Out setting makes shapes disappear during the animation.

C **Fade**: Makes the animation fade in or out.

D **Wipe**: Makes the animation wipe in or out.

E **Motion Ease**: Determines whether the animation accelerates or decelerates.

You can remove a Timeline Effect from an object by selecting the object and choosing Modify > Timeline Effects > Remove Effect. We'll cover editing effects in Exercise 5 of this chapter.

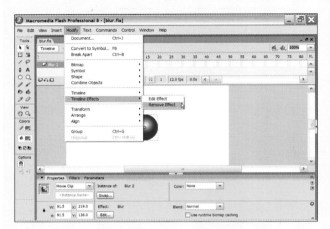

Working with Frames

A lot of the work that you will do in Flash involves using frames, so it is important to develop your frame manipulation skills from the beginning. This exercise helps you learn to work with frames and encourages you to use the shortcut menu and shortcut keys to work more efficiently. You'll also learn how to insert a movie clip into your Flash file.

Start File
↳ 03_002.fla

Final File
↳ 03_002_end.fla

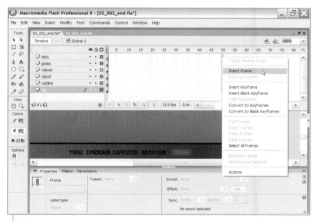

1 Open the start file from the supplementary CD.

2 You will need to add frames 2 to 50 on all layers. Click frame 50 of the text layer to select it. Hold down the Shift key and click on frame 50 of the bg layer, then right-click and select Insert Frame from the shortcut menu.

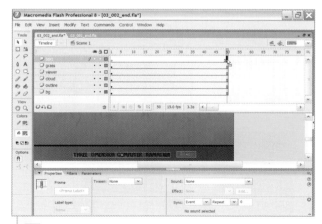

3 We'll need to move the text "THREE DIMENSIONAL COMPUTER ANIMATION" to frame 50 so that it appears briefly before the animation ends. Click on the first frame of the text layer and drag it to frame 50.

- If the frames to be selected are next to each other, either vertically or horizontally, hold down the Shift key and select the first and last frames. All the frames in between will also be selected.

- To select a block of continuous frames, select a frame from one corner of the block. Then hold down the Shift key and select a frame from the opposite corner.

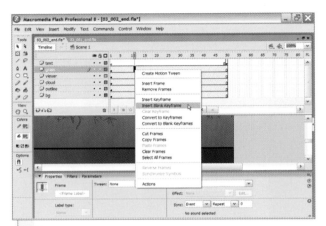

4 The next step is to alter the movie to make the plants along the river's edge disappear in the middle of the animation and appear again towards the end. Right-click on frame 11 of the grass layer and select Insert Blank Keyframe from the shortcut menu. This will remove the content in frame 11 and all subsequent frames. If you had used the Clear Frames command, only the content in the selected frame would have been removed.

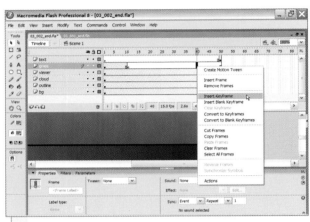

5 To make the plants appear again, right-click on frame 40 and select Insert Keyframe.

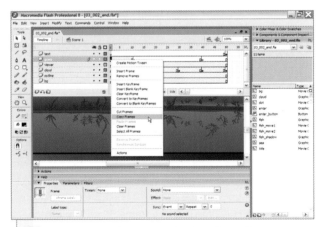

6 Right-click on frame 1 and select Copy Frames.

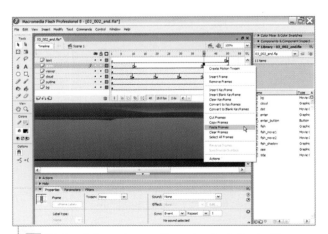

7 Right-click on frame 40 and select Paste Frames. The plants will appear from frame 40 on.

8 In this step, we will animate the sky by making the color change gradually as the movie plays. Start by inserting a keyframe at every tenth frame of the cloud layer. Select frame 50 of the cloud layer and, holding down the Ctrl/Command key, select frames 40, 30, 20 and 10. Press F6 to insert keyframes.

tip >>

Selecting Several Frames at the Same Time: Method 2

- Another way of selecting continuous frames is to click on a frame and, without releasing the mouse, drag the cursor across all of the frames to be selected.

- If the frames are not next to each other, select the first frame or group of frames, hold down the Ctrl/Command key, and select the next frame to add to the selection. You can continue to add frames by holding down the Ctrl/Command key and clicking. If you select the wrong frame, clicking on a selected frame while holding the Ctrl/Command key will clear the selection.

tip >>

Using the Ctrl/Command Key

When you hold down the Ctrl/Command key and move your mouse pointer over a starting or ending keyframe, the pointer turns into a double-headed arrow, indicating that you can add or remove frames to the left or right of the keyframe.

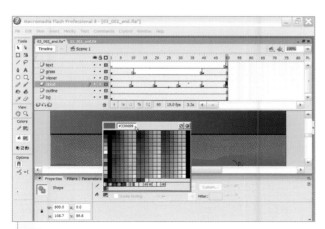

9 Select frame 10 of the cloud layer and click on the sky on the Stage. Check that you selected the sky and not the clouds. You should see a Shape icon in the Properties panel. Click on the Fill Color box in the Properties panel and enter #336699 in the text box to color the sky cobalt blue. Repeat the step on the other keyframes using the following color values: frame 20: #666699, frame 30: #805580, frame 40: #267373, frame 50: #496085.

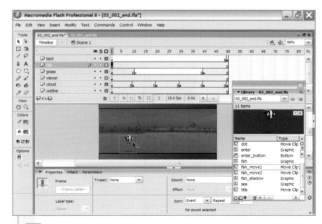

10 We will now add another layer, featuring a fish, to the movie. Select the grass layer and click on the Insert Layer icon (🗐) underneath the bg layer. Double-click on the name of the newly added layer, type in "fish," and press Enter. Press Ctrl-L (Command-L for Macintosh) to open the Library panel. Click on frame 1 of the fish layer and drag the fish_move1 movie clip to the Stage, as shown.

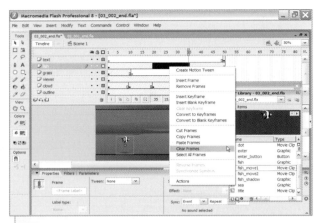

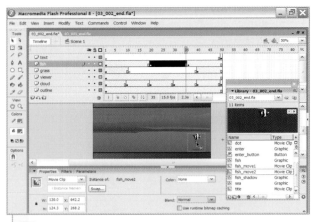

11 Now we'll insert a second movie clip showing the same fish swimming in a different style. Select frames 20 to 35 of the fish layer. Right-click and select Clear Frames from the shortcut menu to delete the content between these frames.

12 Drag the fish_move2 movie clip from the Library panel to the right of the Stage.

13 To test your movie, press Ctrl-Enter (Command-Return for Macintosh). This will open a new window. Close it to return to your movie.

Managing Layer Folders

Start File
— ● 03_003.fla

Final File
— ● 03_003_end.fla

It's possible to work on Flash files that have over 100 layers for a single animation. With that many layers, it's important to be organized and to group layers together into folders. You can treat layer folders in the same way as individual layers. Each time you make a change to a folder, the change is applied to every layer inside the folder.

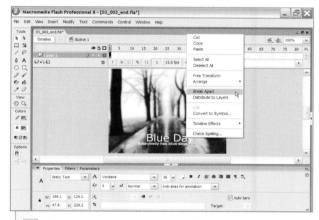

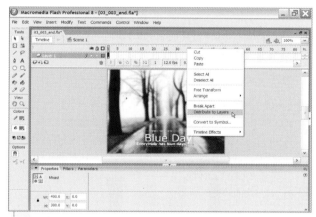

1 When you open the resource file, you should see an image of trees with the phrases "Blue Day" and "Everybody has blue days." Select the text "Blue Day," then right-click and choose Break Apart from the pop-up menu.

2 Select all the objects on Layer 1 using the shortcut Ctrl-A (Command-A for Macintosh). Right-click and select Distribute to Layers from the pop-up menu.

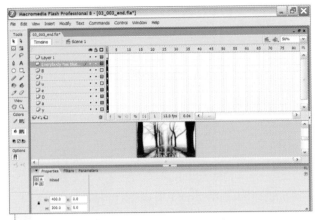

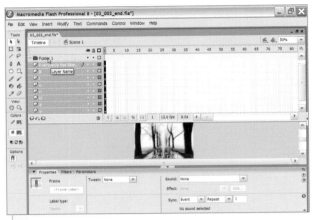

3 All of the objects will be distributed to separate layers. You can see that each of the letters in "Blue Day" has been placed on its own layer. Notice that the text layers have taken their names from the text objects on the layer.

4 The Timeline looks cluttered with so many layers. Let's organize the layers using layer folders. Select the Everybody... layer and click the Insert Folder Layer icon (⬚). You should see "Folder 1" above the layer.

5 Click the Everybody... layer again and, holding down the Shift key, click on the y layer to select all layers with text at the same time. Drag these layers to the new folder.

tip >>

Breaking Apart Text

Applying the Break Apart command once to the text will break up the words into individual letters, while applying the command a second time will turn the letters into shapes.

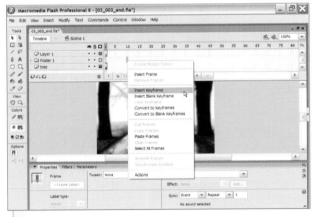

6 Click on the ▽ icon next to the folder to close it. As you can see, storing the text layers in a folder frees up a lot of space in the Timeline. Next, move your mouse over the bottom of the Timeline until you see a double-arrow symbol (⬍). Click and drag the bottom of the Timeline upward so you can give more space to the Stage.

7 Select frame 10 from the layer folder, right-click the frame, and choose Insert Keyframe from the shortcut menu that appears.

tip >>

Dragging Layers within Folders

Layers in the layer folders can be moved around in the same way as layers outside folders. You can drag these layers to change their stacking order or move them out of the layer folder altogether.

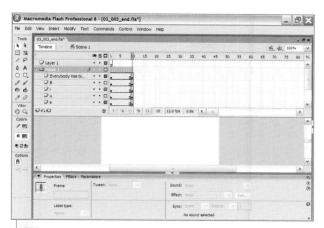

8 Click on the triangle icon (▷) to the left of the layer folder to open it. You can see that the Insert Keyframe command has been applied to all the layers in the folder. This is a quick way of applying the same command (Insert Frame, Delete Frame, Insert Keyframe, etc.) to all of the layers in a folder.

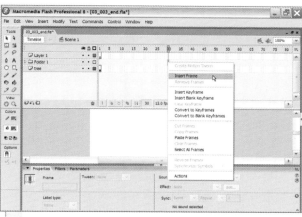

9 Close the folder. This time, select frame 30, right-click, and select Insert Frame.

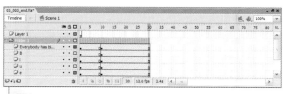

10 When you open the folder, you can see that the command has been applied to the same frame on all of the layers in the folder.

11 With the layer folder selected, click on the Delete Layer icon (🗑) at the bottom of the Timeline.

12 A warning message will appear, stating that by deleting the layer folder, you will also delete the layers within it. Click Yes.

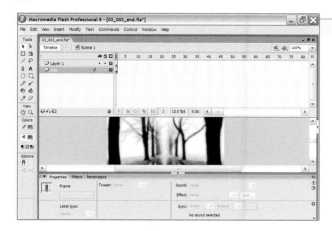

13 The screenshot at left shows that the layer folder and all of the layers within it have been deleted.

Creating and Using Graphic Symbols

Symbols are the backbone of most of the animation that takes place in Flash. Whenever you use a graphic more than once, you should convert it to a symbol. This exercise will help you create a graphic symbol and use instances of it on the Stage.

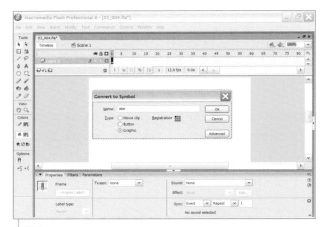

Start File
03_004.fla

Final File
03_004_end.fla

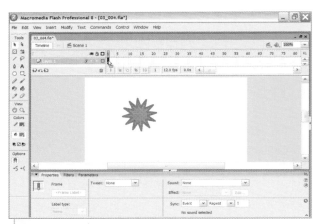

1 Open the start file and select frame 1 in Layer 1 in the Timeline. You can see that all of the sections of the star shape are selected on the Stage.

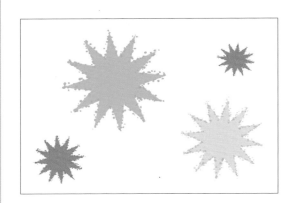

2 Press F8 to open the Convert to Symbol dialog box. Enter the name "star," set the Type to Graphic, and click OK.

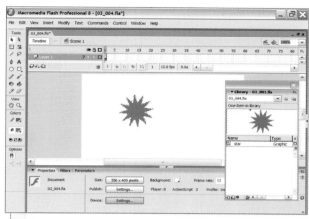

3 The star will be surrounded by a blue square and the Properties panel will display symbol properties.

4 Press Ctrl-L (Command-L for Macintosh) to open the Library panel. You'll see the star symbol in the Library.

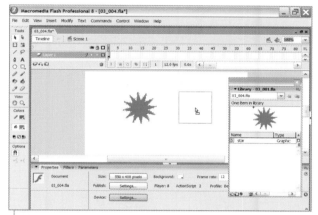

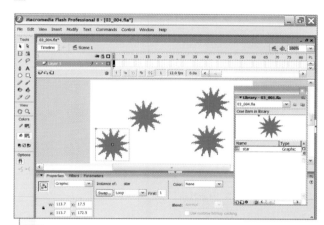

5 Drag the star symbol from the Library onto the Stage.

6 Repeat step 5 until you have four instances of the star symbol on the Stage.

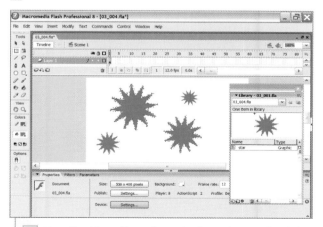

7 Use the Free Transform tool to size each of the instances differently.

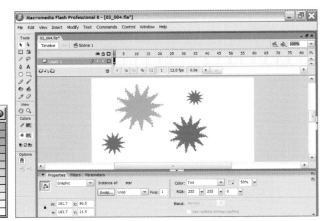

8 Select one of the instances of the star symbol and view the Properties panel. Change the Color setting to Tint, enter a tint color of #FFFF00, and change the Tint value to 50%.

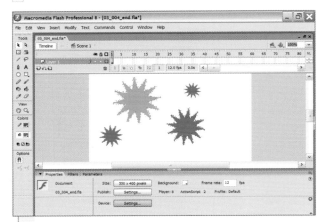

9 The instance should now appear with a different color.

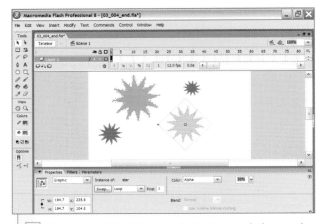

10 Select another of the star instances and change the Color property to Alpha. Set the Alpha value to 30%.

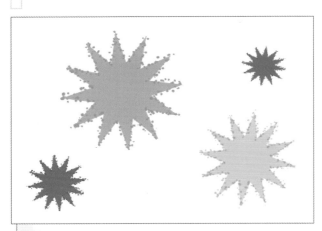

11 Press Ctrl-Enter (Command-Return for Macintosh) to test the movie. When you have finished, you will need to close this window to return to your Flash movie.

106

4 Creating Button Symbols

Button symbols interact with the mouse and have their own Time-line based on how the mouse is being used. In this exercise, we'll create a button symbol and modify instances of it on the Stage.

Start File
→ 03_005.fla

Final File
→ 03_005_end.fla

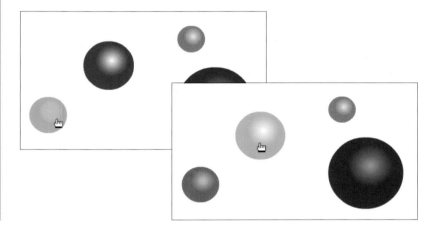

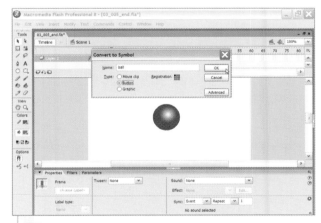

1 Open the start file and select frame 1 in Layer 1 on the Timeline. Press F8 to open the Convert to Symbol dialog box. Enter "ball" for the name, set the Type to Button, and click OK.

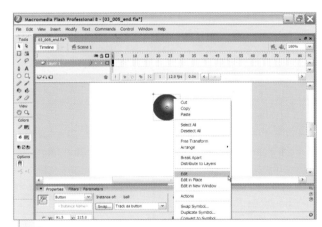

2 Right-click the symbol on the Stage and select Edit from the shortcut menu that appears.

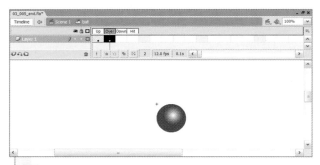

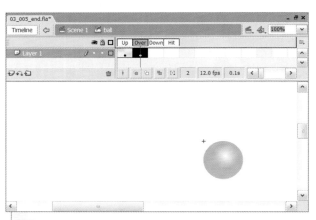

[3] We are now editing the button. Notice that there are four frames in the Timeline. Select the Over frame and press F6 to create a keyframe.

[4] Open the Color Mixer panel to edit the gradient for the fill. With the Playhead on the Over keyframe, change the right point on the gradient bar to an orange color. The ball shape on the Stage should change color.

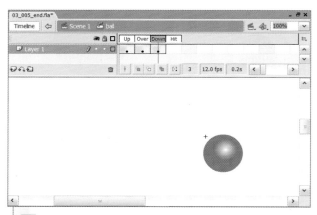

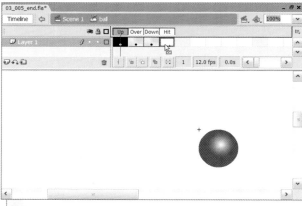

[5] Select the Down frame and press F6 to create a duplicate keyframe from the Over frame. Change the right color point in the gradient bar to a red color, for example #FF0000. Click on the ball to activate the Properties panel. Enter a value of –5 for both the X and Y positions.

[6] Click the Up frame, hold down the Alt/Option key, and drag it to the Hit frame to create a duplicate. The Hit frame sets the clickable area of the button and in this case, we're using the same shape as in the Up frame.

tip >>

Copying Keyframes

You can copy keyframes by clicking and dragging with the Alt/Option key held down. A plus sign appears on the mouse pointer to let you know that the keyframe is being duplicated.

tip >>

The Test Movie Window

You can also choose Control > Test Movie from the menu bar to preview the movie in the Test Movie window.

7 Press Ctrl-Enter (Command-Return for Macintosh) to test the movie. Point to the ball shape and click it. Watch how the button's color changes as you move your mouse over it and click.

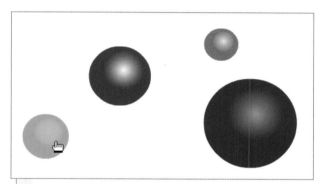

9 Press Ctrl-Enter (Command-Return for Macintosh) to test the movie. Move your mouse over each of the button instances to see the interaction.

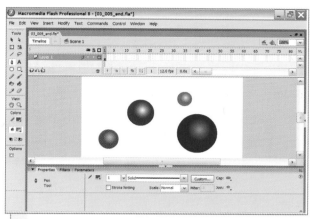

8 Close the Test Movie window to return to Flash. Click Scene 1 in the Timeline to return to the Stage. Click and drag the ball button symbol with the Alt/Option key held down to create a new instance of the symbol. Change the size of the copied symbol as shown and add a tint using the Color setting in the Properties panel. Repeat to add two more instances and add different tints. You should have four different-colored instances on the Stage.

tip >>

Adding Symbols

The Library contains all symbols that are used in the movie. You can use it to locate symbols that don't appear on the Stage. If the symbol is already on the Stage, you can duplicate it by copying and pasting or by dragging with the Alt/Option key held down.

Creating an Animation Using the Blur Timeline Effect

In this exercise, you will learn how to create an animation using the Blur Timeline Effect. You will also learn how to edit the animation by editing both the effect and the frames that create the effect.

Start File

3_006.fla

Final File

03_006_end.fla

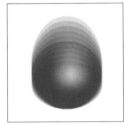

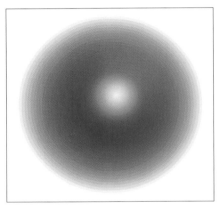

 Open the start file. You should see a ball shape on the Stage.

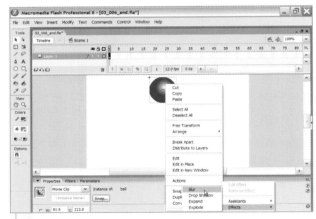

 Right-click the shape and select Timeline Effects > Effects > Blur from the shortcut menu.

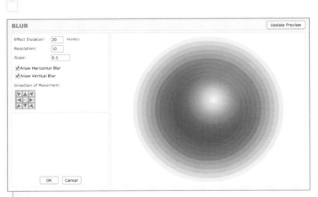

 In the Blur dialog box, enter the following settings: Effect Duration: 20 frames, Resolution: 10, Scale: 0.5. Click the Update Preview button to see the effect.

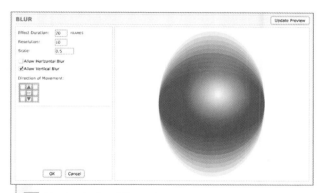

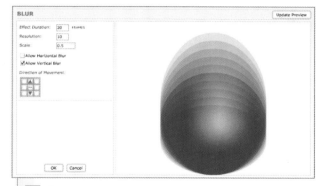

4 Uncheck the Allow Horizontal Blur option. The left and right buttons will be removed from the Direction of Movement section. Press Update Preview to preview the animation in the Blur dialog box.

5 Click the upward-pointing arrow in the Direction of Movement option, then update the preview. The animation should show the object expanding at the top and then gradually disappearing.

6 Press OK to add the Timeline Effect to the object on the Stage. The object won't look any different but the Timeline will show 20 frames.

tip >>

Direction of Movement

Use the arrow keys to determine the direction of movement within an animation. For example, click the arrow shown here to move the Blur effect to the right.

7 Select the object on the Stage. The Properties panel shows that it is a graphic symbol and that it is an instance of Blur 1 with the effect Blur.

8 Press Ctrl-L (Command-L for Macintosh) to open the Library panel. The Blur 1 symbol and the Effects Folder have been added to the Library. If you open this folder, you will see that it contains Symbol 1.

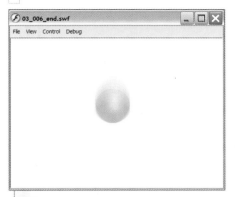

9 Press Ctrl-Enter (Command-Return for Macintosh) to test the movie. Check to see that the Blur effect has been applied to your object.

Editing the Blur Timeline Effect

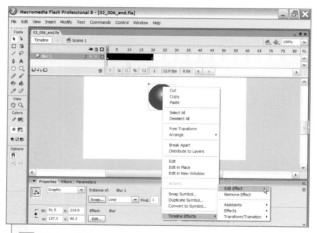

1 Right-click the circle symbol on the Stage and select Timeline Effects > Edit Effect from the shortcut menu.

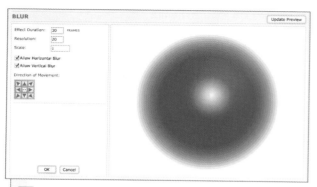

2 The Blur dialog box will appear. Make the following changes: Effect Duration: 30 frames, Resolution: 20, Scale: 1. Ensure that both Allow Horizontal Blur and Allow Vertical Blur are checked and click the center box for Direction of Movement. Click OK to apply the changes.

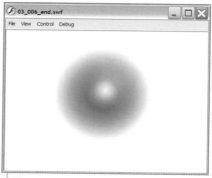

3 Press Ctrl-Enter (Command-Return for Macintosh) to test the movie.

Editing the Blur Animation on the Timeline

If you edit the frames of the animation on the Timeline, you will no longer be able to update the Timeline Effect using the Blur dialog box.

Final File
● 03_007_end.fla

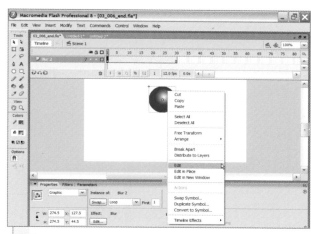

1 Right-click the symbol instance and choose Edit from the shortcut menu.

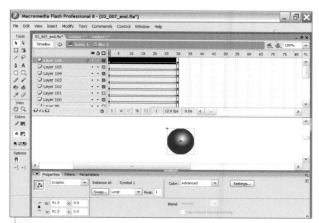

2 You should see the Effect Settings Warning. Click OK to continue editing the object.

tip >>

Effect Settings Warning

This warning message will appear whenever you try to edit an object that has a Timeline Effect applied. If you click OK to continue, you will no longer be able to modify the Timeline Effect using Edit Effect.

3 When you edit the animation, the view will change to the symbol edit window. The layers and frames used to create the animation effect will be displayed.

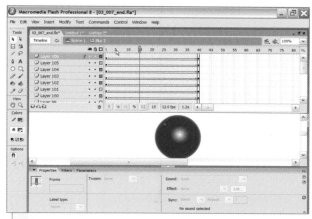

4 Click on frame 5 in the Timeline and press F5 to insert frames until you have 40 frames on all layers.

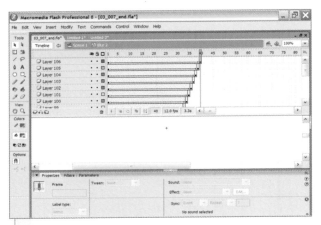

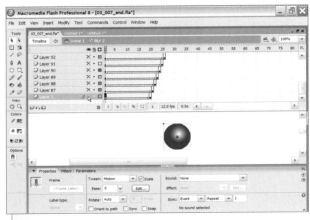

5 Move to the top layer in the Timeline. Click the layer beneath and press Shift-F5 to remove one frame. Move to the layer beneath and remove two frames. Continue until you have achieved a staggered effect as shown above. As you work on lower frames, you may want to Shift-click to select multiple frames before pressing Shift-F5.

6 Click the Layer 1 layer on the left of the Timeline. Click on the Show/Hide option while holding down the Alt/Option key to hide all other layers.

tip >>

Alt/Option-Clicking a Layer Option

If you select a layer by clicking the layer name, then hold down the Alt/Option key and click a layer option (Show/Hide, Lock/Unlock, or Outline), the option will be applied to all layers other than the selected layer.

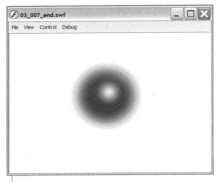

7 Press Ctrl-Enter (Command-Return for Macintosh) to test the movie. Check to see that the animation has been edited.

Using Timeline Effects to Create Text Animations

You can also apply Timeline Effects to text objects to create simple but effective text animations. These effects look best with short, large blocks of text.

Using the Blur Timeline Effect

Start File

03_009.fla

Final File

03_009_end.fla

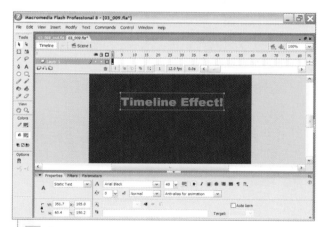

1 Open the start file. The Properties panel will show that the object is a text object.

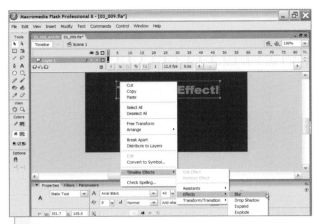

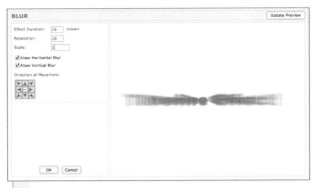

2 Right-click the text and choose Timeline Effects > Effects > Blur.

3 In the Blur dialog box, set the Resolution to 10, set the Scale to 1, and make sure the center arrow at the bottom is selected for Direction of Movement. Click OK to apply the effect.

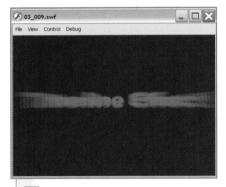

4 Press Ctrl-Enter (Command-Return for Macintosh) to preview the results.

Using the Expand Timeline Effect

Start File
03_009.fla

Final File
03_010_end.fla

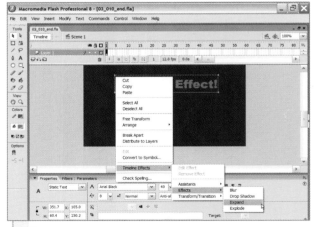

1 Open the start file. Right-click the text and select Timeline Effects > Effects > Expand.

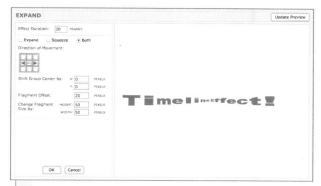

2 In the Expand dialog box, select the Both radial button and set "Change Fragment Size by" to Height: 50 and Width: 50. Click OK to apply the effect.

3 Press Ctrl-Enter (Command-Return for Macintosh) to preview the results.

Using the Explode Timeline Effect

Start File
03_009.fla

Final File
03_011_end.fla

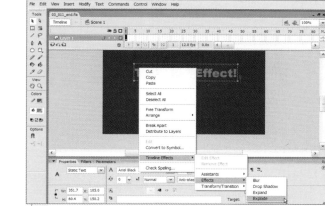

1 Open the start file, right-click on the text, and select Timeline Effects > Effects > Explode.

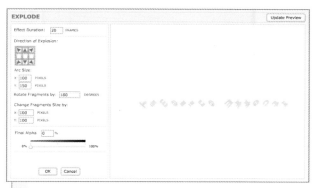

2 Enter the following settings: Rotate Fragments by: 180, Change Fragments Size by: X: 100, Y: 100. Click OK.

3 Press Ctrl-Enter (Command-Return for Macintosh) to test the movie.

Chapter 4

Animating in Flash

The word "animation" originates from the Latin word for soul, anima, and the word animatus, which means to move to action and give life to. In this chapter, we,ll bring together everything you have learned in the preceding pages and put theory into practice. It's time to animate! You will have the chance to create your own animations in this chapter using frame-by-frame and motion-tweened animation.

Animation Methods

There are three methods for animating in Flash: frame-by-frame, tweening, and ActionScript. In Chapter 4 we'll cover the basics for each method and then move on to exercises that cover frame-by-frame and tweening. ActionScript is covered in depth in the next chapter.

Frame-by-Frame Animation

Frame-by-frame animation is the most straightforward method for creating animations. As the name implies, you create a different still image for each frame in the animation. Another name for frame-by-frame animation is cell animation, which was the method used to produce animations in older movies and TV shows. Although this technique is great for creating detailed animations and provides the most creative control, it is very laborious and time-consuming. See Exercise 1 for a demonstration of frame-by-frame animating in Flash 8.

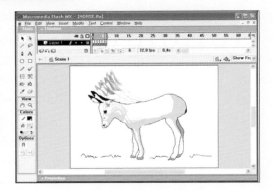

Tweened Animation

In tweened animation, you create a starting keyframe and an ending keyframe and let Flash fill in the frames between. Flash automatically calculates the in-between frames based on the images in the two keyframes. This is much faster than frame-by-frame animation.

There are two types of tweening: shape tweening and motion tweening. Before you tween an animation, you have to specify the kind of tweening you are going to perform. First, select the frames you want to tween. Then select Motion or Shape from the Properties panel.

Shape Tweening

You've probably seen examples of morphing effects in science fiction movies. Morphing is a common technique for showing transformations (a human changing into an animal, for instance). Although you can't recreate the sophisticated 3D effects you see in the movies with Flash, you can turn one object into another with shape tweening. You can tween shapes to change their size, shape, color, and position.

120

If shape tweening is applied correctly, the tweened frames in the Timeline will be colored light green, and a solid arrow will appear between the keyframes. Where there is a mistake, you will see a dotted arrow across the frames in the Timeline. For a more detailed exploration of shape tweening in Flash, see Exercise 4.

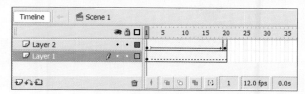

Motion Tweening

With motion tweening, you can make an object move along the path you select. You can also change its properties by manipulating the object's ending frame. You can tween the position, size, and rotation for different symbol instances, groups, and text. You can also tween colors.

As with shape tweening, you will see a solid arrow across the tweened frames when the motion tweening is applied correctly. If you make mistakes, such as omitting an ending keyframe, you'll see a dotted arrow in the Timeline. See Exercises 2 and 3 for step-by-step instructions covering motion tweening in Flash. Also check out the following: Let's Go Pro exercises: The Revolving Earth and Rotating an Object.

note >>>

To tween the colors of groups or text, you must turn them into symbols first.

Animation Using ActionScript

This final animation technique does not interpolate the frames to create animation. Instead, it uses ActionScript, the scripting language of Flash. This enables you to create complex animations with small file sizes. However, because you need to have a basic understanding of the ActionScript language, it will take more effort to master than tweening.

note >>>

You will learn more about ActionScript in Chapter 5.

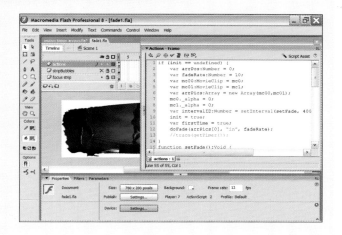

1

Creating Line Effects Using Frame-by-Frame Animation— A Glowing Earth

The animation we will be creating in this example changes the color of a different line in every frame so it draws the viewer's gaze from the outside in. As animation techniques go, frame-by-frame animation is the most time-consuming of all. This example provides an excellent opportunity for you to review the concepts you have learned so far, and to gain a more concrete understanding of timelines, frames, and animation.

Start File
> 04_001.fla

Final File
> 04_001_end.fla

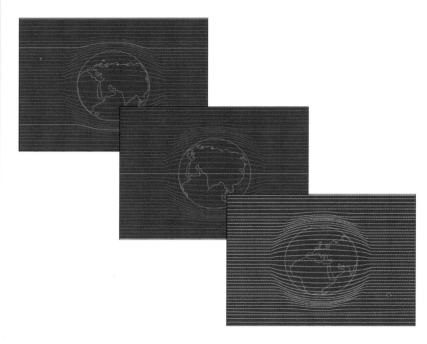

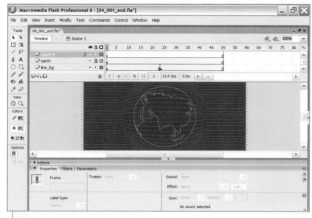

1 Choose File > Open to open the resource file. Select the earth layer and click the Add Layer icon (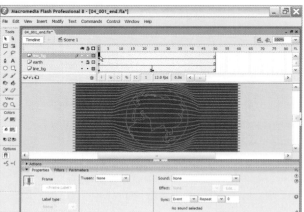) to add a new layer.

2 Select frame 1 of the line_bg layer. With the Alt/Option key pressed down, drag it to the new layer to make a copy. After frame 1 is copied onto the new layer, the name of the layer changes to line_bg. Now you'll have two layers with the same name.

3 While holding down the Alt/Option key, click on the Lock/Unlock icon of the new line_bg layer to lock all of the other layers.

tip >>

Three Ways of Selecting Several Frames at Once

- If the frames you want to select are side-by-side, click on the first frame and then the last frame while holding down the Shift key.

- Another way is to click on the first frame and, without releasing the mouse, drag to the last frame.

- If the frames are not side-by-side, hold down the Ctrl/Command key and click each frame you want to select one at a time.

The method that you choose is a matter of personal preference.

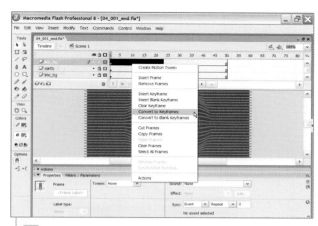

4 Select frames 1 to 22 of the new line_bg layer, right-click, and choose Convert to Keyframes from the pop-up menu. You can see from the Timeline that the frames have been converted into keyframes. Click on the grey Pasteboard to deselect the lines.

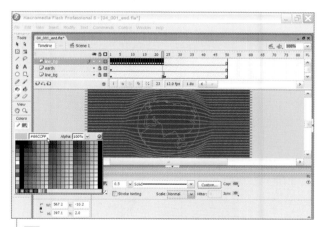

5 Select the Ink Bottle tool (🖋) from the Tools panel and set the line color to #66CCFF, as shown.

6 Notice that your cursor has turned into an Ink Bottle pointer. Click frame 1 and check that all the lines are deselected. Next, click the topmost and bottommost lines to change the line color. Select frame 2 and click on the second topmost and bottommost lines to change their color.

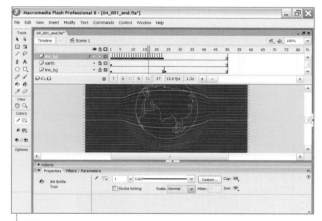

7 Repeat step 6 for all the frames. The objective is to change the color of the lines until you reach the center. After a while, you might forget which line you were working on, so you may want to move the Playhead from frame to frame to check your work.

You can access the Undo command by selecting Edit > Undo from the menu bar or by using the shortcut Ctrl-Z (Command-Z on a Macintosh). The Undo command can reverse up to 100 previous actions. If you cancel a step by mistake, you can recover it with the Redo command: Choose Edit > Redo from the menu bar or use the shortcut Ctrl-Y (Command-Y on a Macintosh).

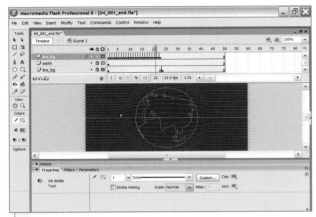

8 By the time you get to frame 21, you should have one line left. As in the preceding steps, use the Ink Bottle tool (▣) on the final line to change the color.

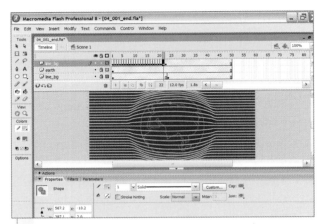

9 Change the Stage size to 50% from the drop-down box at the top-right corner of the Timeline. Then select frame 22. With all of the lines on frame 22 selected, set the line color to #66CCFF.

You can open the Properties panel by choosing Window > Properties or by using the shortcut Ctrl-F3 (Command-F3 on a Macintosh).

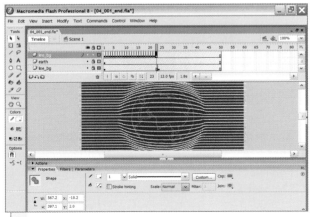

10 Select frame 23. With all of the lines on frame 23 selected, change the line color to white (#FFFFFF) and the line thickness to 1 in the Properties panel.

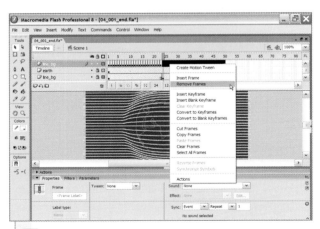

11 Select frames 24 to 50 on the top line_bg layer. Right-click and select Remove Frames, or press Shift-F5 to delete the selected frames.

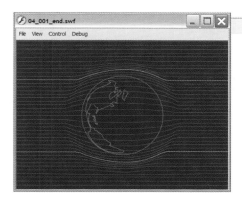

12 Let's test what we've done. Choose Control > Test Movie from the menu bar or press Ctrl-Enter (Command-Return for Macintosh). The test will show you how the SWF movie file will look when it is played. The animation grabs the attention of the viewer by focusing the eye on the center of the converging lines. If you spotted some mistakes during the test, make the necessary corrections and test the movie again.

tip >>

Make a Habit of Saving Your Work!

If you don't make a habit of saving your work periodically, you could lose everything in the event of a power failure or surge. Your computer could also crash, especially when you're working in a memory-intensive graphics program like Flash. To avoid disaster, get into the habit of periodically pressing Ctrl-S (Command-S on a Macintosh) to save your work.

Start File
04_002.fla

Final File
04_002_end.fla

The Revolving Earth

You might be thinking that creating this movie involved drawing each and every frame to simulate the movement of the rotating earth. It could be done that way, but animating frame by frame is time-consuming and the resulting file size is enormous.

In this section, we will learn an easier way to work using motion tweening. For starters, remember that it's a good idea to plan beforehand so you can create an animation efficiently and effectively.

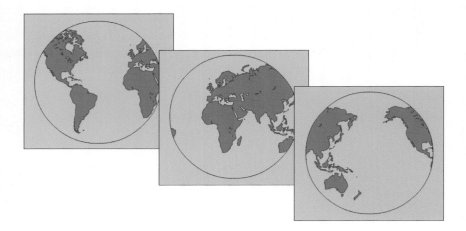

01 Open the completed file from exercise 1, 04_001_end.fla, to see how the movie was made. Holding down the Alt/Option key, click the Lock/Unlock icon ( ) of the earth layer to lock all the other layers. On the Stage, right-click on the globe and select Edit from the pop-up menu.

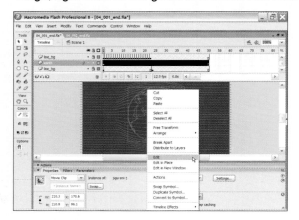

02 Move the Playhead from frame to frame and you will observe that every frame contains a different stage of the earth's rotation. If you were asked to create the rotation stages to fill all 23 frames, you'd probably close this book! But don't worry, there is an easier way to get this done.

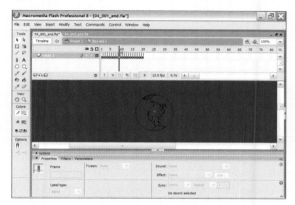

03 Open the resource file 04_002.fla. You will see a flat, 2D image of the earth. We are going to add a mask layer to this image so that only part of it is visible. To create a mask layer, add a new layer above the earth_plane layer and name it "circle." Then lock the earth_plane layer.

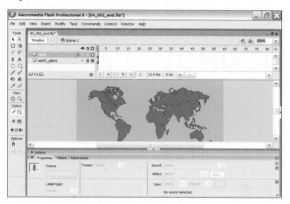

04 Select the Oval tool (◎) from the Tools panel and draw a circle on the map as shown. Make sure the circle has both a line and a fill. Choose a black color for the line. The fill color doesn't matter as we'll make it transparent. The line will be visible when we've finished.

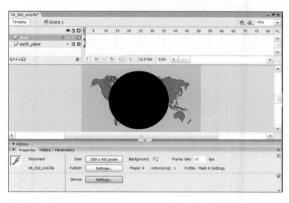

05 Use the Selection tool to select the circle, then press Shift-F9 to open the Color Mixer panel. To see the map area covered by the circle, set the Alpha value to 0% and click on the Stage. The circle's fill will become transparent and you'll only be able to see the line.

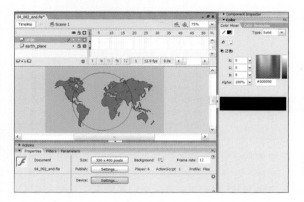

tip >>

Mask Layers

In Flash, you can use a filled shape on a mask layer to show selected portions of the image underneath. For example, if you place a filled circle on a mask layer, only the areas beneath the circle will show through from the underlying image. Areas outside the circle are hidden.

In the globe tutorial, you have to make the flat, 2D map look like a globe. To do so, you must use a mask to reshape the map image.

06 Select the circle layer and press Ctrl-F8 (Command-F8 for Macintosh) to open the Create New Symbol dialog box. Name the symbol "clarity_circle" and click OK to enter symbol editing mode. Clicking Scene 1 in the Timeline will return you to the main Stage.

note >>>

In the Create New Symbol dialog box, you can choose from the three symbol types: movie clip, button, and graphic. Each type of symbol has distinct characteristics. See Chapter 3 for additional details.

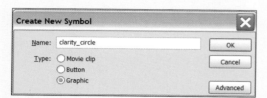

07 Let's make a copy of the circle layer. First, add a new layer. Then, with frame 1 of the circle layer selected, hold down the Alt/Option key and drag it to the first frame of the new layer. The new layer's name automatically changes to "circle." The new circle layer will be used as an outline of the globe.

08 Click the Lock/Unlock icon (🔒) of the earth_plane layer while holding down the Alt/Option key. This locks all the other layers. Double-click on the map so you can edit the graphic. Select frame 1 and press Ctrl-G (Command-G for Macintosh) to group all the objects on this layer together.

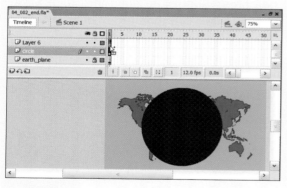

tip >>

Why Do I Need to Register the Circle as a Symbol?

A symbol is a master copy of a graphic, button, or movie clip that is stored in the Library. Once you turn an object into a symbol, it can be used over and over again. To use a symbol, you drag a copy, called an instance, from the master copy in the Library. When you use symbols, you reduce the file size of your document. This is because Flash stores the symbol only once, regardless of how many instances of it you use in your animation. Even if you create 100 instances, the computer only needs to save one symbol.

If you intend to play your Flash animation on the Web, a small file size is essential for speed. As a rule, if you intend to use the same object more than once, it is a good idea to turn it into a symbol first. You will save a lot of time while editing, as you only need to edit the symbol in the Library to update all instances automatically. In this example, we saved the circle as a symbol because we will be using it as a mask element and as the outline of the globe.

09 With the map selected, hold down the Ctrl/Command key and drag a copy out to one side. Check that the two images line up horizontally and make sure that the spacing between them is adequate.

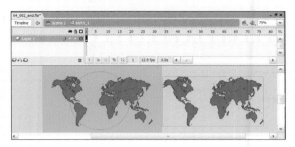

10 Click Scene 1 in the Timeline to return to the main Stage. Selecting the 30th frame on all the layers, press F5 to insert frames. Next, select only frame 30 of the earth_plane layer, and press F6 to insert a keyframe.

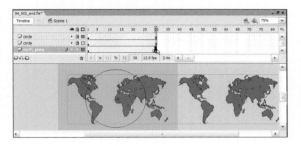

11 Move the Playhead to frame 1, positioning the map face-to-face with the circle on the Stage. See the figure below.

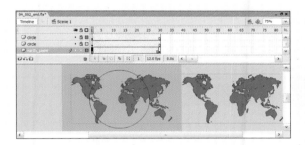

12 Move the Playhead to frame 30 and move the map to the left of the Stage. Move the image of the map so that its right side lines up with the left side of the map in frame 1.

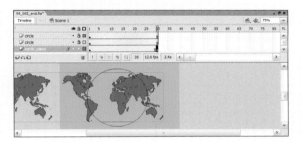

13 Right-click on any frame between 1 and 29 on the earth_plane layer, and choose Create Motion Tween from the pop-up menu. Frames 1 to 29 will be colored purple in the Timeline after the motion tweening is applied.

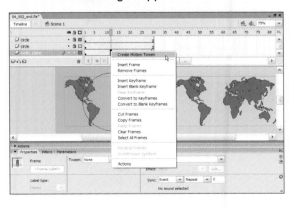

14 Right-click on the circle layer right above the earth_plane layer and select Mask from the pop-up menu.

15 Press Ctrl-Enter (Command-Return for Macintosh) to test the movie. You should see an animation of a revolving globe. You may need to adjust the placement of the graphics on the Stage to make the animation run smoothly.

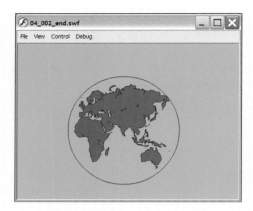

Simulating Camera Movement with Motion Tweening

In this tutorial, you will motion tween a drawing of a room to simulate camera movement and changes in perspective. To visualize the movie, imagine that you are a movie director looking through the camera's viewfinder. The movie starts with a close-up of a picture hanging above the bed, then the camera moves to the top-left corner of the room and back out of the room.

Start File
— 04_003.fla

Final File
— 04_003_end.fla

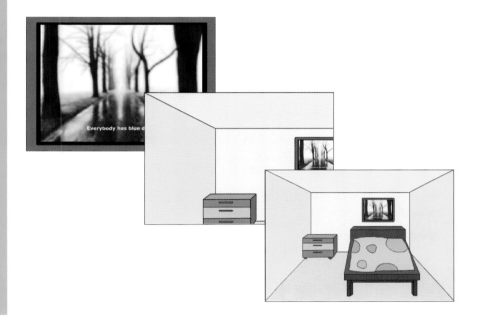

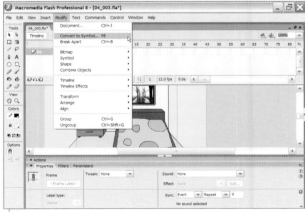

tip >>

About Motion Tweening

Motion tweening is easy. All you need to do is create the first and last frames of an animation and Flash automatically fills in the in-between frames. When used creatively, motion tweening can create a wide range of animation effects, making changes to space, size, color, and transparency. To motion tween, the object must be a symbol, text, or a grouped object.

1 Use the Ctrl-O (Command-O for Macintosh) shortcut to open the start file, then press Ctrl-Enter (Command-Return for Macintosh) to test the movie. You can see that the picture hanging above the bed is animated. It is a movie clip symbol, so you can animate it separately from the rest of the movie.

2 You need to convert the objects on the Stage into symbols in order to apply motion tweening. Click on frame 1 of the bg layer to select all the objects in this frame, then choose Insert > Convert to Symbol from the menu bar or press F8.

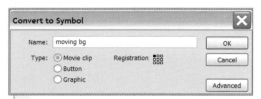

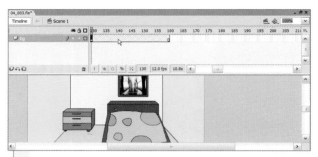

3 Enter "moving bg" in the Name field, set the Type to Movie Clip, and click OK.

4 Select frame 160 of the bg layer and press F5 to insert frames. With a frame rate of 12 fps, the entire movie will run for 13.3 seconds. Now hold down the Ctrl/Command key and select frames 50, 90, and 130. Release the Ctrl/Command key and press F6 to insert the keyframes that you'll use in the animation.

tip >>

Setting the Registration Point for a Symbol

The registration point of a symbol is effectively the symbol's center of gravity. It's the primary axis point for the symbol as it's being animated, and your results will vary significantly if you change the location of the registration point.

You can only set the registration point for a symbol in the Convert to Symbol dialog box. By default, the registration point is set in the middle of the symbol. To change its location, click on one of the points on the registration indicator.

When you use actions in your animations, you should note that the default registration point is at the top-left coordinate (0,0).

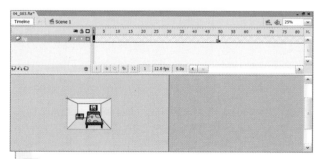

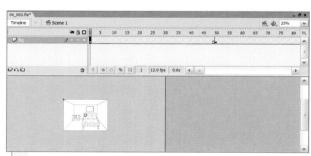

5 The movie starts with a close-up of the picture hanging above the bed. In the following steps, you'll have to expand the picture to cover the Stage completely. First, select frame 1 and reduce the size of the Stage to 25%.

6 As you can see, the room covers the entire Stage. Click on the Show Outline icon (▣) for the bg layer to show only the room's outline and reveal the Stage underneath.

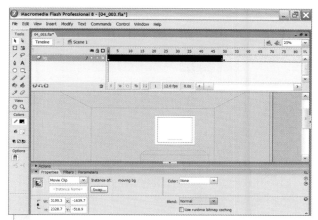

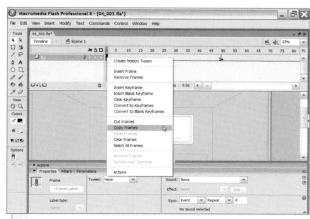

7 Select the Free Transform tool (⊞). Holding down the Shift key, click and drag the bounding box handles of the symbol outwards. You may need to use the Selection tool to reposition the symbol. When you're finished, the picture should be expanded to fit the Stage perfectly, as shown above.

8 You'll have to make a copy of frame 1 on frame 50 so the picture is displayed over all 50 frames. Right-click frame 1 and select Copy Frames from the pop-up menu.

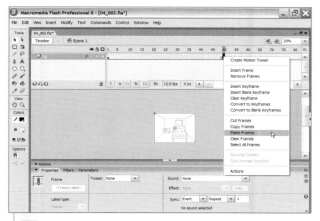

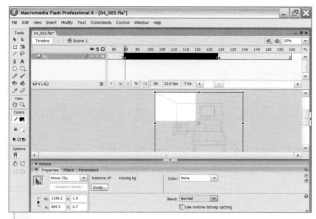

9 Right-click frame 50 and select Paste Frames from the pop-up menu. Another way of making a copy is to select frame 1 and drag it to frame 50 while holding down the Alt/Option key. At a frame rate of 12 fps, the picture is shown for about three seconds.

10 In frame 90, the movie will display the upper-left corner of the room. Select frame 90 and use the Free Transform tool (⊞) to expand the room. Position it as shown here.

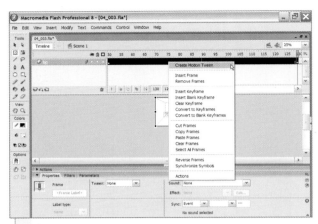

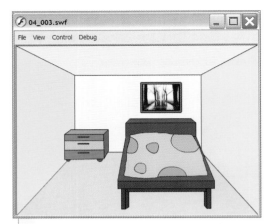

11 Now that you have created the contents in the keyframes, it's time to animate! Select frames 50 to 130, as shown here, then right-click and choose Create Motion Tween from the pop-up menu.

12 On the Timeline, the motion-tweened frames will be colored light purple. Press Ctrl-Enter (Command-Return for Macintosh) to test the movie and check that the animation runs correctly.

tip >>

Tweening Shortcut

In the preceding steps, you had to tween from frames 50 to 90 and then from frames 90 to 130. Since you had keyframes on frames 50, 90, and 130, the instructions were for you to select frames 50 to 130 and then tween everything in one step. But actually, you don't have to select all the frames between frames 50 and 130. There's an even faster way.

You only need to select the center keyframe (frame 90) and at least one frame each from the left and right. You can select frames 80 to 100, for example, and still tween everything between frames 50 and 130 by applying a motion tween. You can save a lot of time with this shortcut.

note >>>

Movie clips, like the picture in the tutorial above, run on their own Timeline and do not follow the main Timeline.

Motion guide layers are used to determine the path of an object during its animation. They are used in more complicated animations where the object doesn't move in a straight line. Lines drawn on the motion guide layer determine the direction of movement for the object. In this example, we will create a motion guide to determine the direction that a boy takes on his snowboard.

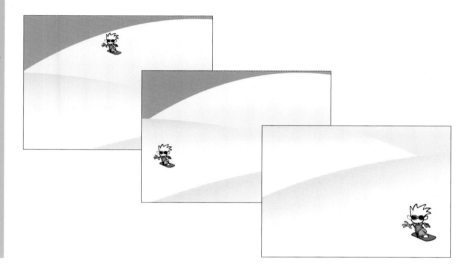

Using Motion Guides

Motion guides work best using single, smooth lines without breaks. The object being animated must be aligned with the start and end points of the path in the keyframes at the beginning and end of the animation. When the object is motion tweened, it will follow the line on the motion guide layer.

Start File
- 04_005.fla

Final File
- 04_005_end.fla

1 Press Ctrl-O (Command-O for Macintosh) to open the start file.

2 Select the boy layer and click the Add Motion Guide icon ( ). Then lock the boy layer by clicking on the Lock icon ( ).

tip >>

Shortcut to Open Files

Hit Ctrl-O (Command-O on a Macintosh) to open files.

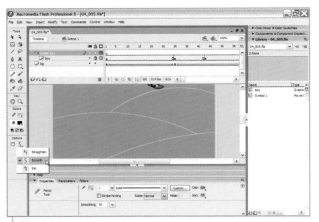

3 Click the bg layer and select the Outline option (□). Choose the Pencil tool (✏) and select the Smooth option (S.) from the Toolbox.

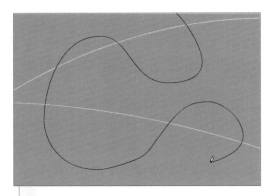

4 Draw a curve on the Guide: boy layer similar to the one shown here. Then lock the Guide: boy layer.

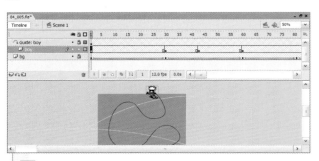

5 Select the boy layer and use F6 to insert keyframes at frames 30, 43, 60, and 100.

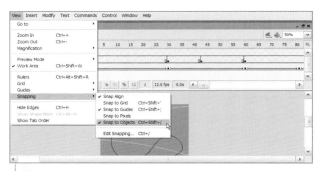

6 Choose View > Snapping and make sure that the Snap to Objects option is checked.

7 Make sure that all layers are locked except the boy layer.

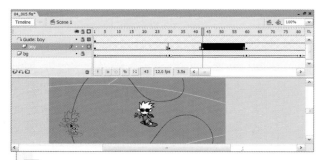

8 For each section of the animation, the boy symbol must be snapped to the line drawn in the Guide: boy layer. The boy symbol contains a small circle with a cross; this is the center point. When you start positioning the boy, make sure that the center point is snapped to the line.

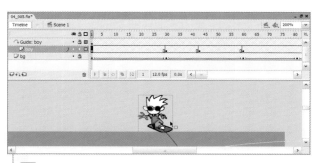

9 Click on frame 1 and use the Free Transform tool to make the boy symbol smaller. Drag the symbol to the beginning of the motion path and make sure that it snaps into place.

136

10 Snap the boy symbol to the hill outline in frame 30 and make the symbol slightly larger with the Free Transform tool.

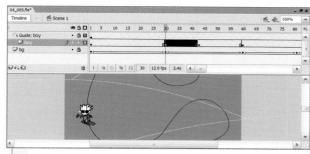

11 Snap the boy in frame 43 to the motion guide on the left and make it slightly smaller.

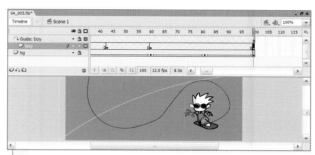

12 At frame 60, snap the object to the motion guide at the right of the Stage. Finally, snap the boy to the end of the motion guide at frame 100 and increase the size of the object.

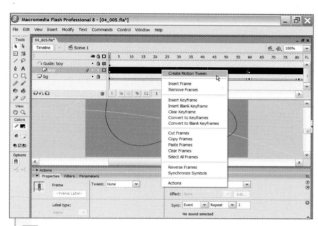

13 Select frames 1 to 99 of the boy layer, then right-click and choose Create Motion Tween.

14 Select a frame between frames 30 and 43 of the boy layer and check the Orient to path option in the Properties panel.

tip >>

Orient to Path

This option aligns the baseline of the object with the motion guide.

15 The animation is split into four sections. Select a frame from each section and set the Ease values in the Properties panel as follows: Frames 1-29: –100, Frames 30-42: 100, Frames 43-59: –100, Frames 60-100: 100. A negative value eases the animation in, so that it starts slowly and speeds up—in other words, the animation accelerates. A positive value, or easing out, does the opposite.

16 Press Ctrl-Enter (Command-Return for Macintosh) to preview the movie.

Let`s Go Pro!

Start File
04_006.fla

Final File
04_006_end.fla

Rotating an Object

An object can be rotated during motion tweening. The effect this has depends on the center point of the object, which you can set while editing it. In the following examples, you will change the center point of an object to see how this affects the animation.

Center Point Set in the Center of the Object

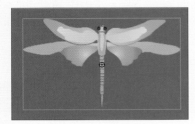

01 Open the start file, select frame 20, and press F6 to insert a keyframe.

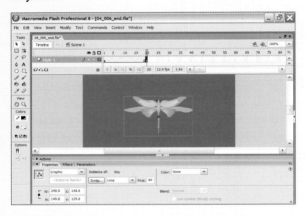

02 Click frame 1 and, in the Properties panel, set the Tween to Motion and set Rotate to CW.

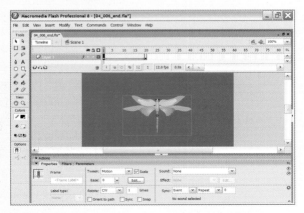

138

03 Press Ctrl-Enter (Command-Return for Macintosh) to test the movie, then watch how the object rotates.

Center Point Set Outside of the Object

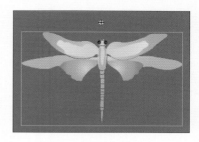

Final File
● 04_007_end.fla

01 Open the start file and double-click the symbol to edit it on the Stage. Drag the symbol so that the center point appears above the blue box.

02 Click the blue arrow (⬅) in the Timeline to return to the Stage, select frame 20, and press F6 to insert a keyframe.

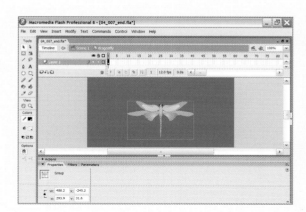

03 Click frame 1 and, in the Properties panel, set the Tween to Motion and Rotate to CW.

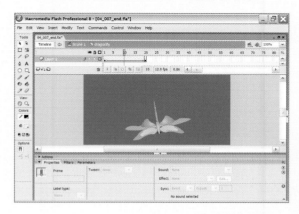

04 Press Ctrl-Enter (Command-Return for Macintosh) to test the movie. Notice that the object rotates along a different path in this animation.

4 Shape Tweening

Shape tweening is used to change the shape of an object. This is also called morphing. Shape tweening is quite different from motion tweening; rather than symbols, it uses shapes drawn with the drawing tools or symbols that have been broken apart into shapes with the Break Apart command.

Final File
04_008_end.fla

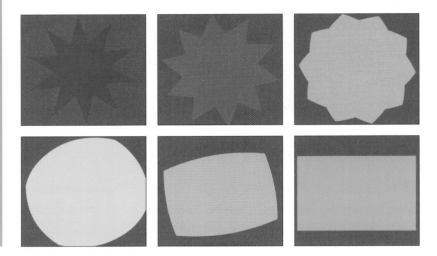

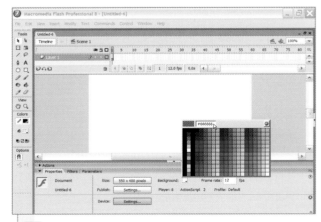

[1] Create a new movie using the Ctrl-N (Command-N for Macintosh) shortcut and select Flash Document from the General tab. Set Background to #666666 in the Properties panel.

[2] Choose the PolyStar tool (⬡) from the Tools panel and click the Option button in the Properties panel to open the Tool Settings dialog box. Set Style to star, set Number of Sides to 10, and click OK.

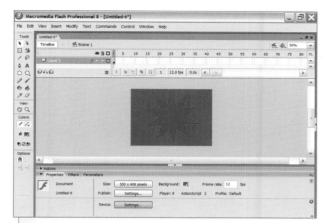

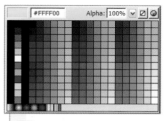

3 In the Tools panel, set the stroke color to no color () and the fill color to #9900FF. Draw the shape shown above.

4 Insert a blank keyframe at frame 20 by pressing F7.

5 Select the Oval tool and set the stroke color to no color ( ) and the fill color to #FFFF00.

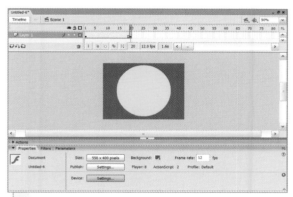

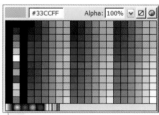

6 Draw a circle on the Stage in the same position as the star.

7 Insert a blank keyframe at frame 40 using the F7 key.

8 Select the Rectangle tool and set the fill color to #33CCFF.

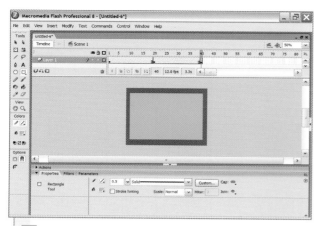

9 Draw a rectangle on the Stage in the same position as the circle.

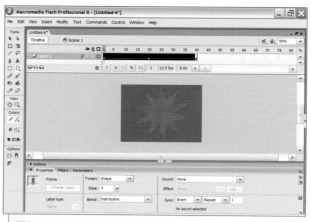

10 Select frames 1 to 39, and set the Tween to Shape in the Properties panel.

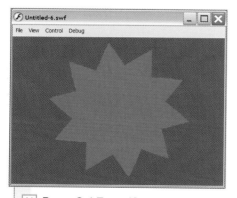

11 Press Ctrl-Enter (Command-Return for Macintosh) to test the movie.

142

5

E-Card Animation

In the last exercise of this chapter, we will use a combination of techniques to create an e-card. We'll use motion tweening to move the background elements and a motion guide layer to simulate the erratic movements of a butterfly. In addition, you'll learn how to fade in a block of text and add a drop shadow filter to an object.

Start File
04_009.fla

Final File
04_009_end.fla

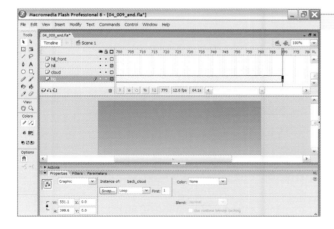

1 Open the start file and insert 350 frames on the bg layer. You can do this by clicking the last frame and pressing the F5 key.

2 Select the cloud layer and increase the total number of frames in this layer to 350. Insert keyframes into frames 75 and 213 with the F6 key.

tip >>

Inserting a Large Number of Frames

When you look at the Timeline, it appears to only contain a fixed number of frames. However, as you add frames, the length of the Timeline will increase. Click the last frame you can see and press F5 to insert frames. The Timeline will extend and you will then be able to add more frames with the F5 key.

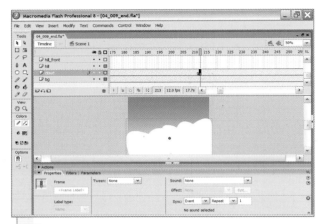

3 Select frame 213 and drag the back_cloud symbol from below the Stage so that the top of the symbol reaches the middle of the Stage.

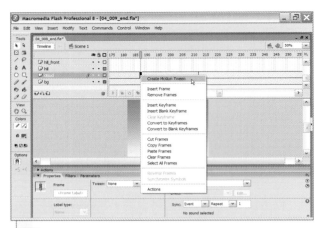

4 Right-click between frames 75 and 212 of the cloud layer and select Create Motion Tween from the pop-up menu.

5 Select the hill layer and increase the total number of frames to 350. Add keyframes to the layer at frames 60 and 204.

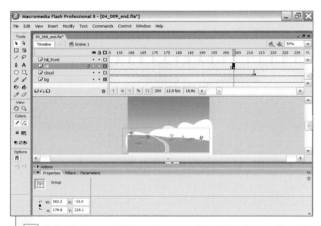

6 Select frame 204 and move the objects on the hill layer slightly below the back_cloud symbol on the cloud layer.

7 Right-click between frames 60 and 204 of the hill layer and add a motion tween.

8 Select the hill_front layer and increase the total number of frames to 350 with the F5 key. Insert keyframes at frames 96 and 240.

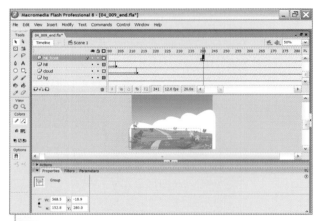

9 Select frame 204 of the hill_front layer and position the objects slightly below the hill layer objects.

10 Right-click between frames 96 and 240 and add a motion tween.

11 Select the cloud_front layer and use the F5 key to increase the total number of frames to 350. Insert a keyframe at frame 20 with the F6 key.

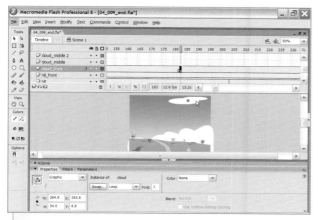

12 Insert a keyframe at frame 183 and move the cloud symbol onto the Stage.

13 Right-click between frames 22 and 183 and add a motion tween.

14 Using the same approach, add a motion tween to the cloud_middle layer between frames 1 and 209 so that the cloud moves onto the Stage. Increase the number of frames to 350. Repeat the process for the cloud_middle 2 layer, adding a motion tween between frames 6 and 292 to move the cloud onto the Stage.

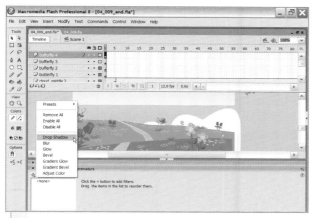

15 If you have Flash Professional, you'll also be able to add a drop-shadow effect. Click frame 1 in the butterfly 4 layer and select the Filters tab in the Properties panel. Click the Add Filter button (⊞) and choose Drop Shadow. Change the strength setting in the Filters panel to 30% so that the shadow isn't too dark.

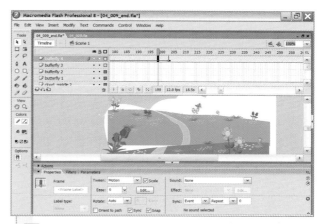

16 Right-click on frame 1 to copy the frame and paste it at frame 204. Reposition the butterfly on top of the flower and create a motion tween. Extend the frames on this layer to 350.

17 Select the butterfly 2 layer and drag frame 1 to frame 214. Extend the number of frames to 350 using the F5 shortcut key.

18 Add a Drop Shadow filter to the butterfly, changing the strength to 30%.

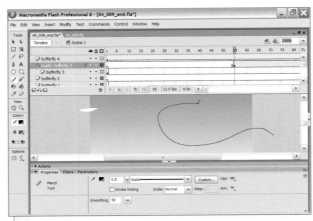

19 Insert a keyframe at frame 243 and position the butterfly on top of the pink flower. Create a motion tween.

20 Select the butterfly 3 layer and click the Add Motion Guide (⬡) icon. This creates a new layer that will be used to guide the motion of the butterfly symbol.

21 Press F7 at frame 55 on the Guide: butterfly 3 layer to insert a blank keyframe. Use the Pencil tool to draw the line shown above. This will become the flight path for the butterfly.

22 Select frame 1 of the butterfly 3 layer and add a 30% Drop Shadow filter to the butterfly using the Filters tab in the Properties panel.

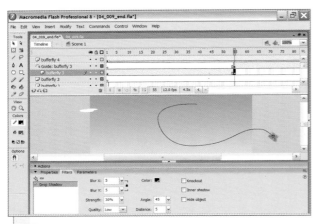

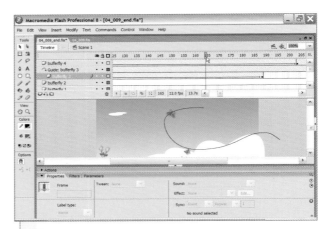

23 Press the F6 key at frame 55 of the butterfly 3 layer to insert a keyframe, then drag the butterfly symbol to the start of the motion guide.

24 Add another keyframe at frame 189 and drag the butterfly to the end of the motion guide. Add a motion tween. If you drag the Playhead, you will see the butterfly following the path on the motion guide layer. Extend the number of frames to 350.

25 Use the Selection tool to select frame 1 of the butterfly 1 layer, then add a 30% Drop Shadow filter. Drag it to frame 263. Set the Alpha value of the butterfly symbol to 0%.

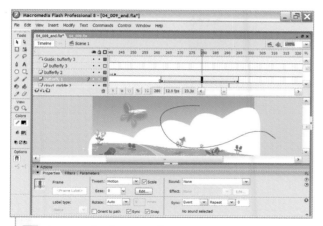

26 Insert a keyframe at frame 295 and set the Alpha value to 100%. Create a motion tween between frames 263 and 295. Increase the number of frames to 350. Animating the Alpha value creates a fade-in effect.

27 Select the butterfly 4 layer and add a layer. Name it "text." Click on frame 1.

28 Click the Text tool (A) in the Tools panel and make the following changes in the Properties panel: Font: Arial Black, Font Size: 20, Font Color: #660000.

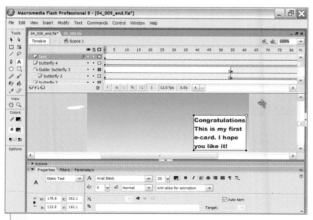

29 Click on the Stage and add the following text: "Congratulations. This is my first e-card. I hope you like it!"

30 Click frame 1 of the text layer and drag it to frame 300. You have completed the card. Use the Ctrl-Enter (Command-Return for Macintosh) shortcut to test the movie.

Chapter | 5

Advanced Animation Techniques

In the last chapter, you learned to create animations using frame-by-frame animation, shape tweening, and motion tweening. In this chapter, we'll look at some advanced animation techniques including animating masks, working with movie clip Timelines, and using ActionScript to create non-linear animations.

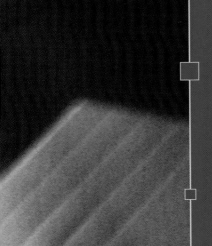

Animating Masks

As discussed in Chapter 4, a mask layer contains an object that hides or reveals objects on the layer below. Areas covered by the mask layer will be visible in the final animation, while uncovered areas won't. In this section, you will learn how to animate a mask, which can create some interesting effects.

Creating an Animated Mask

To mask an object, create a layer above the object and draw a shape. It doesn't matter what color you choose for the fill of the masking object, because the shape will be hidden in the final animation. Right-click the layer containing the mask and choose Mask from the pop-up menu.

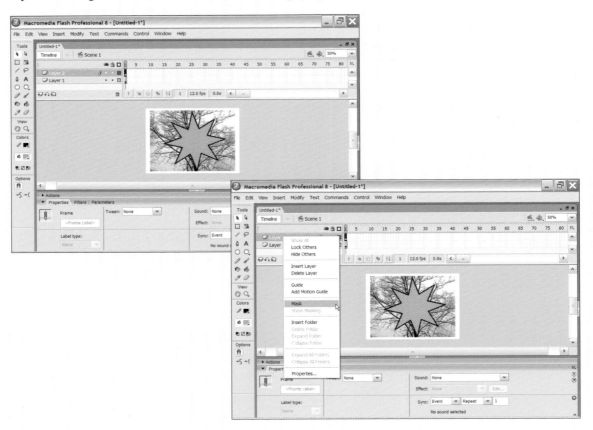

After masking, both layers are locked and the layer to be masked is indented in the Timeline below the mask layer.

You can use a shape or a movie clip for the masking object. If you choose a movie clip, you'll be able to create an animated mask. Movie clip symbols run within their own Timeline, which is completely separate from the main Timeline. You can animate movie clip symbols using exactly the same techniques that you've learned so far. In a way, it's like creating an animation within an animation.

When you create an animation using a mask, there are two things you need to keep in mind to ensure that the animation works properly. First, if there are two or more groups or instances in the mask layer, the animation may recognize only one group or instance or none at all. Second, if you want to use text as a mask, you must break the text apart into shapes. The shortcut to do this is Ctrl-B (Command-B on a Macintosh), and you'll need to apply it twice to break the text into individual letters first, then into shapes.

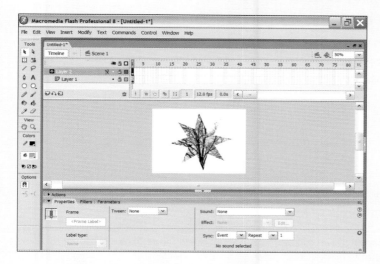

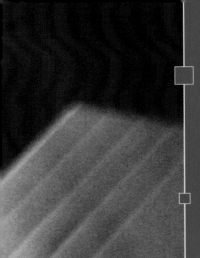

Using Behaviors

A ctionScript is Flash's own programming language, and advanced Flash designers use it to create complicated movies. When you first get started, you will probably want to use behaviors, which generate ActionScript code for you.

Understanding the Behaviors Panel

The Behaviors panel, which you can bring up with Shift-F3 or by selecting Window > Behaviors, makes it easy to apply advanced actions to movie clips, sound, and video. First select the object that is the target of the behavior, then choose the behavior to apply.

Movie Clip Behaviors

The Behaviors panel contains twelve behaviors that relate specifically to movie clips. The details of each of these behaviors are covered in the following table.

Behaviors to Control Movie Clips

Behavior	Purpose	Information Required
Bring Forward	Brings the target movie clip one position higher in the stacking order.	Instance name of movie clip.
Bring to Front	Brings the target movie clip to the top of the stacking order; the clip appears on top of all other clips on the Stage.	Instance name of movie clip.
Duplicate Movieclip	Duplicates a movie clip.	• Instance name of movie clip to duplicate. • X-offset and Y-offset (position of duplicate from original in pixels).
Goto and Play at frame or label	Plays a movie clip from a specified frame.	• Instance name of movie clip to play. • Frame number or label to play from.
Goto and Stop at frame or label	Stops a movie clip, optionally moving the Playhead to a specified frame.	• Instance name of target clip to stop. • Frame number or label to stop at.
Load External Movieclip	Loads an external SWF file into a target movie clip.	• URL/filename of external SWF file. • Instance name of movie clip or screen in which to load the SWF file.

Behavior	Purpose	Information Required
Load Graphic	Loads an external JPEG file into a movie clip.	• Path and filename of JPEG file. • Instance name of movie clip in which to load the graphic.
Send Backward	Sends the target movie clip one position lower in the stacking order.	Instance name of movie clip.
Send to Back	Sends the target movie clip to the bottom of the stacking order (i.e., the clip appears underneath all other clips on the Stage).	Instance name of movie clip.
Start Dragging Movieclip	Starts dragging a movie clip.	Instance name of movie clip.
Stop Dragging Movieclip	Stops the dragging action.	N/A
Unload Movieclip	Removes an SWF file loaded with the Load Movie behavior or action.	Instance name of movie clip to unload.

Using Behaviors to Load Images

Flash allows you to load an image while a movie is playing using the Movieclip > Load Graphic behavior. This is normally used to load an image when a button is clicked. The image is then loaded into an existing movie clip that is already positioned on the Stage.

The Load Graphic Dialog Box

Ⓐ Enter the URL or filename of the image to be loaded.

Ⓑ Select the movie clip instance into which the graphic is to be loaded.

Ⓒ Click here to enter the movie clip based on its relative path.

Ⓓ Click here to enter the movie clip based on its absolute path.

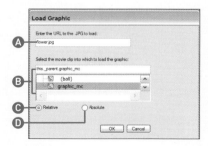

note >>>

Relative and Absolute Paths

Relative paths can only be used for movie clips that are contained within the current movie clip. You will probably want to select this option when working with behaviors, as it allows for more flexibility when reorganizing complicated movies. For example, if you move the parent movie clip to a new Flash document or place it inside another movie clip, you won't need to rewrite the paths in your behaviors. See the following section, devoted to Actionscript, for additional details regarding relative and absolute paths.

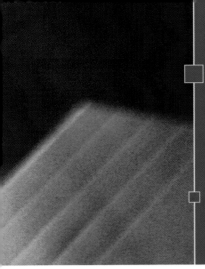

ActionScript

ActionScript is made up of a series of actions written in the Actions panel, and it is important to become familiar with this area of Flash. You can only explore the most advanced possibilities of Flash---including interactivity--- through the use of ActionScript.

Understanding the Actions Panel

You can open the Actions panel by pressing the F9 key or by selecting Window > Actions. The actions for the selected frame, button, or movie instance will be displayed.

Most people starting out with ActionScript should click the Script Assist button (Script Assist) so they can get help writing ActionScript code. If you click this button, the top of the Actions panel will change. Now, whenever you add an action, this top section will show the options that you need to enter.

The Key Areas of the Actions Panel

The Actions panel is made up of several areas. The image on the right shows the Actions panel with the Script Assist button selected.

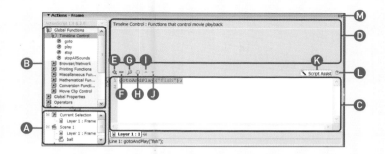

A Script Navigator: The Script Navigator contains information about a symbol, instance, or scene name. You can use it to display scripts that relate to the selected item.

B Actions Toolbox: The toolbox contains all actions organized into categories that are displayed in a tree structure. You can either double-click an action or drag it to the Script window.

C Script Window: The Script window contains the actions that make up your ActionScript. Actions are added by selecting them from the action toolbox or by clicking the Add a New Item to the Script button (⬚).

D Script Assist Area: The contents of this area will change depending on what action is selected in the Script window.

E Add a New Item to the Script: Click the plus sign (⬚) and navigate to the appropriate action to add it to the script.

F Delete the Selected Action: Click the action you want to delete and press the minus sign (⬚) to remove the selected action.

G Find: Find can be used to search for and replace specific words in the Actions panel.

H Insert a Target Path: Insert a Target Path shows a tree structure listing the path to all instances on the Stage. A path allows you to specify which object you'll work with. In Script Assist mode, this button only becomes active when you select certain options.

I Move the Selected Action Up: Click this button to move the selected action up one line.

J Move the Selected Action Down: Click this button to move the selected action down one line.

K Script Assist: Click the button to enter Script Assist mode. In this mode, you can select the appropriate actions and fill in the details at the top of the window. This mode is recommended for people who aren't familiar with writing ActionScript.

L Help: Brings up the Help panel.

M **Options Menu:** The Options menu shows options for the Actions panel, including Go to Line, Find and Replace, Import Script, and Export Script.

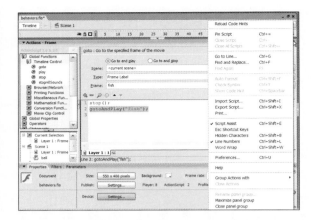

Placing ActionScript within a Movie

There are three places in a movie where you can add ActionScript: a frame, a button, or a movie. Your choice will depend on the effect that you are trying to achieve. Your actions can be entered into these areas using the Actions panel.

Actions added to a frame are often used to determine how a movie will play. You can only add actions to a keyframe. To add actions, click the keyframe and press F9 to display the Actions - Frame panel.

Adding actions to a frame with Script Assist

An action associated with a button usually controls what happens when the button is clicked. You can add ActionScript by selecting the button instance on the Stage and pressing the F9 key to show the Actions - Button panel.

Adding actions to a button with Script Assist

156

Movie clip instances often use ActionScript to make something happen when the mouse pointer moves over the instance. Select a movie clip instance on the Stage and press the F9 key to show the Actions - Movie Clip panel.

Adding actions to a movie clip with Script Assist

Selecting Paths

Paths are critical in Flash, as they allow you to refer to specific symbols while ActionScripting. Essentially, once you define an action, you'll use paths to let Flash know which object(s) the action should be applied to. There are two methods for providing path information to Flash, relative and absolute.

Relative

Relative target paths describe symbol locations relative to other objects in the Flash file structure. In plain English, you might say that Symbol A is contained within Symbol B, for instance. Of course, ActionScript doesn't use plain English, so there are several keywords that are used in relative paths. If a symbol appears inside another symbol, you would refer to the parent symbol using the keyword "_parent". You can use the word "this" to refer to the symbol itself. The word "_root" refers to the main Timeline of the current movie. See the ActionScript samples throughout the book to get a better feel for how relative paths are written.

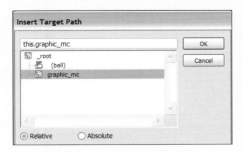

Absolute

Absolute target paths refer to symbols by describing their positions in relation to the main Timeline. These paths start with the Timeline and describe each "step" to the location of the desired symbol. Each part of the path is separated by dots. For example, if you want to refer to a movie with the instance name "ball_mc" inside another clip called "game_mc" on the main Timeline, you would use the absolute path "_level0.game_mc.ball_mc".

157

Actions can control the way a movie plays. The most commonly used actions are those that control frames, such as play(), stop(), gotoAndStop(), and gotoAndPlay(). These commands allow you to play frames in any order instead of relying on the Timeline to play them one at a time (in sequence).

Action	Effect
play()	Plays the movie from the current frame.
stop()	Stops the movie at the current frame.
gotoAndPlay()	Moves to the specified frame and plays the movie.
	Examples: gotoAndPlay(10) Moves to frame 10 and plays the movie. gotoAndPlay("start") Moves to the frame labeled "start" and plays the movie.
gotoAndStop()	Moves to the specified frame and stops playing the movie.
	Examples: gotoAndStop(10) Moves to frame 10 and stops playing the movie. gotoAndStop("start") Moves to the frame labeled "start" and stops playing the movie.

Setting Movie Clip Properties with Actions

Characteristics of a movie clip, such as its size, height, and position on the Stage, can also be controlled using ActionScript. These characteristics are referred to as the properties of a movie clip. All properties in ActionScript have a name that starts with the underscore character (_). You can change a movie clip's properties by referring to its instance name in the Properties panel.

There are two types of movie clip properties: those that you can view or get properties for (i.e., read-only) and those that you can both read and set (i.e., read-write).

All movie clip instances on the Stage have X and Y coordinates, width, height, object size, and xscale/yscale properties. ActionScript can read and set these properties as part of an animation.

The following table shows a list of the commonly used properties and their characteristics.

Property	Get	Set	Explanation
_x	yes	yes	Indicates the X coordinate of the movie clip instance on the Stage (from left to right, starting from the left edge of the Stage).
			Examples: ball._x = 200; Sets the X coordinate of the ball movie clip instance to 200 pixels from the left of the Stage. ball._x += 200; Increases the X coordinate of the ball movie clip by 4 pixels.
_y	yes	yes	Indicates the Y coordinate of the instance on the Stage (from top to bottom, starting from the top edge of the Stage).
			Examples: ball._y = 200; Sets the Y coordinate of the ball movie clip instance to 200 pixels from the top of the Stage. ball._y += 4; Increases the Y coordinate of the ball movie clip by 4 pixels.
_width	yes	yes	Indicates the width of the movie clip instance.
			Examples: ball._width = 100; Sets the width of the ball movie clip instance to 100 pixels. ball._width -=10; Reduces the width of the ball movie clip instance by 10 pixels.
_height	yes	yes	Indicates the height of the movie clip instance.
			Examples: ball._height = 100; Sets the height of the ball movie clip instance to 100 pixels. ball._height -=10; Reduces the height of the ball movie clip instance by 10 pixels.
_alpha	yes	yes	Indicates the transparency of the movie clip instance. The Alpha property can be a value from 0% to 100%. A value of 0 is invisible, while a value of 100 is opaque.
			Examples: ball._alpha -= 10; Reduces the Alpha value of the ball movie clip instance by 10.
_rotation	yes	yes	Indicates the clockwise rotation of the instance in degrees.
			Examples: ball._rotation += 5; Rotates the ball movie clip instance by 5 degrees clockwise.
_visible	yes	yes	Indicates the visibility of the instance; value is either "true" or "false."
			Examples: ball._visible =false; Setting the _visible property to "false" hides the ball movie clip instance. **Note**: The instance will be visible on the Stage and will only be hidden when the movie is tested.

Other Movie Clip Properties

Property	Explanation
_currentframe	Shows the number of the current frame in the movie clip.
_frameloaded	Shows how many frames in the movie clip have been loaded.
_name	Refers to the instance name of the movie clip.
_target	Specifies the target path of the movie clip.
_totalframes	Shows the total number of frames in the movie clip.
_url	Shows the URL of the SWF file from which the movie clip was loaded.
_xmouse	Shows the X coordinate of the mouse cursor.
_ymouse	Shows the Y coordinate of the mouse cursor.
_xscale	Specifies the size using the horizontal scale of the movie.
_yscale	Specifies the size using the vertical scale of the movie.

Dragging a Movie Clip

The startDrag() and stopDrag() actions allow you to drag a movie clip around the Stage using your mouse. These actions allow the user to interact with the Flash movie and are useful in creating games and customized mouse cursors. The startDrag() and stopDrag() actions can also be used to create moveable menu panels.

Once a startDrag() action is applied to a movie clip instance, viewers will be able to drag it around the Stage until they apply a startDrag() action to a different instance or until they activate the stopDrag() action. You can only drag one movie clip at a time.

Action	Explanation
startDrag()	Allows a movie clip instance to be dragged by the mouse; requires the instance name of the movie clip.
	Examples: startDrag("fish") The startDrag() action is applied to the fish movie clip instance on the Stage. **startDrag("fish", true)** A value of "true" means that the center of the movie clip is locked to the center of the mouse pointer. **StartDrag("fish",true, 50, 50, 200, 200)** Specifying rectangular coordinates keeps the movement of the movie clip within that area. If you don't specify coordinates, the movie clip can be moved anywhere on the Stage.
stopDrag()	Ends the drag action that was started with the last startDrag() action; does not require the instance name of the movie clip.

Button Event Handlers

Event handlers allow Flash to respond to events such as the user clicking or moving a mouse over an object. An event handler determines what happens when the event takes place. For example, the On Release event could be used to say that when a button is clicked, a specific frame of the movie is played.

Actions are applied to button instances using the following format:

```
on (Event){
 //do some actions
}
```

tip >>

Writing Notes into ActionScript

Lines starting with // are comments and won't be processed by Flash. You can use them to write yourself notes about the ActionScript without affecting the movie.

There are eight button event handlers that you can use to control your movie.

Event	Event Happens When:
press	The button is pressed while the pointer is over the button's hit area.
release	The button is released while the pointer is over the button's hit area.
releaseOutside	The button is released while the pointer is outside the button's hit area.
rollOver	The pointer is moved over the button's hit area.
rollOut	The pointer is moved from the button's hit area to outside of the button's hit area.
dragOver	The pointer is moved over the button's hit area while the mouse button is held down.
dragOut	The pointer is moved from the button's hit area to outside of the hit area while the mouse button is held down.
keyPress "<>"	A specified key on the keyboard is pressed.

1

Creating a Bouncing Ball Movie Clip

In this section, we will create a movie clip symbol that includes a bouncing ball animation. We will also animate the movie clip symbol on the main Timeline. In effect, we will be creating a double animation.

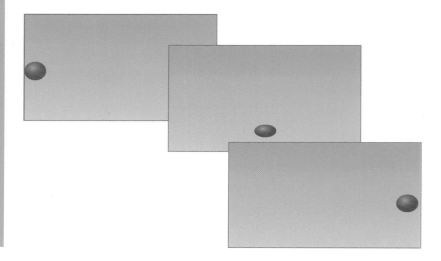

Start File
05_001.fla

Final File
05_001_end.fla

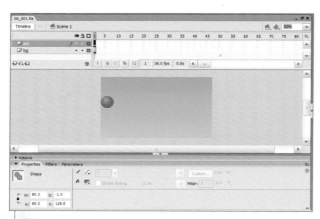

1 Open the start file and select the Shape object in the ani layer.

2 Press the F8 key to open the Convert to Symbol dialog box. Set the Name to "ball," set the Type to Movie Clip, and click OK.

3 Select the ball symbol on the Stage and press F8. In the Convert to Symbol dialog box, enter the Name "ball_updown," set the Type to Movie Clip, and click OK. You have now created a ball_updown movie clip that contains the ball movie clip.

162

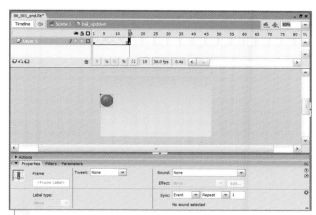

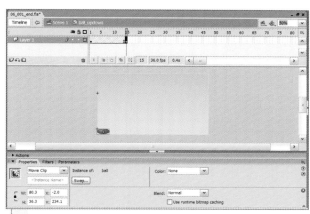

4 Double-click the ball_updown symbol on the Stage to enter symbol editing mode. You are now editing the Timeline of the movie clip, not the main Timeline. Select frame 15 on Layer 1 and press F6 to insert a keyframe.

5 At frame 15, move the ball symbol to the bottom of the Stage and use the Free Transform tool (⊞) to shorten and widen the ball as shown.

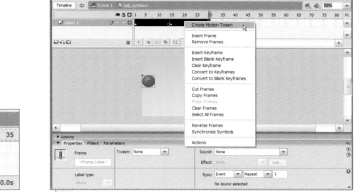

6 Select frame 1 of Layer 1, hold down the Alt/Option key, and drag the keyframe to frame 30.

7 Select frames 1 to 29, then right-click and select Create Motion Tween from the shortcut menu.

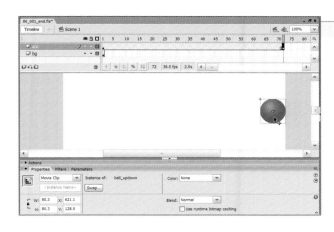

8 Click Scene 1 to return to the main Timeline. Select frame 72 of the ani layer and press F6 to insert a keyframe. Hold down the Shift key and move the ball_updown symbol to the right edge of the Stage as shown.

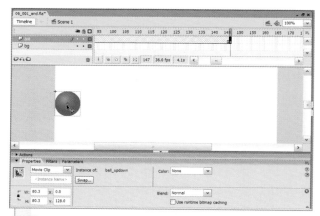

9 Select frame 147 of the ani layer and press F6 to insert a keyframe. Hold down the Shift key and move the ball_updown symbol to the left edge of the Stage as shown.

10 Select frame 147 of the bg layer and press F5 to insert frames. Motion tween frames 1 to 146 of the ani layer. (You also could have copied frame 1 of the ani layer and pasted it into frame 147.)

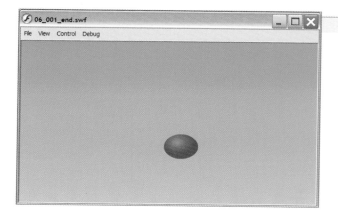

11 Press Ctrl-Enter (Command-Return for Macintosh) to test the movie. The up and down movement is on the movie clip's Timeline, while the right to left movement is on the main Timeline.

2

Animating Masks

In this exercise, we'll animate layer masks to provide transitions between different bitmap images.

Final File
05_002_end.fla

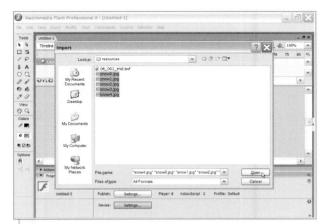

1 Use the Ctrl-N (Command-N for Macintosh) shortcut to bring up the New Document dialog box, then choose the Flash Document option. Press Ctrl-R (Command-R for Macintosh) to open the Import dialog box. Hold down the Shift key and select all the files from snow0.jpg to snow4.jpg. Click Open to import the files to the Stage.

2 Click the Stage and press the Size button in the Properties panel. Set the Dimensions to 500 width and 375 height, set the background color to #000000 (black), and click OK.

3 Zoom out and drag a selection box to select all of the images on the Stage.

4 Press Ctrl-K (Command-K for Macintosh) to open the Align panel. Press the To stage button and click the Align horizontal center and Align vertical center icons to center the images on the Stage. Close the Align panel.

tip >>

Align/Distribute to Stage Button

When you click the To stage button, the options in the Align panel will be applied relative to the size of the Stage. The button will remain pressed until it is clicked again.

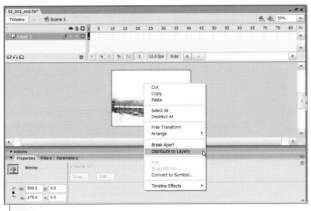

5 Making sure that all of the images are still selected, right-click and choose Distribute to Layers.

6 Delete Layer 1 and drag the layers into the following order from bottom to top: snow0.jpg, snow1.jpg, snow2.jpg, snow3.jpg, and snow4.jpg.

7 Hold down the Alt/Option key and click the Show/Hide option on the snow1.jpg layer. All layers except the snow1.jpg layer will be hidden.

8 Select the image in the snow1.jpg layer and press F8. Change the Name to snow1 and the Type to Movie Clip. Click OK.

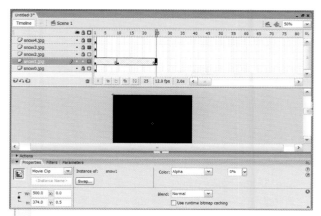

9 Insert keyframes at frame 10 and frame 25. Open the Properties panel and set the Alpha value of the instance on frame 25 to 0%.

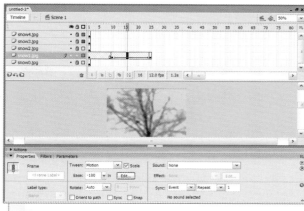

10 Click between frames 10 and 24, go to the Properties panel, and set the Tween to Motion and the Ease to −100.

11 Hold down the Alt/Option key and click the Show/Hide option of the snow1.jpg layer to show all the layers. Click the snow0.jpg layer and drag frame 1 to frame 10.

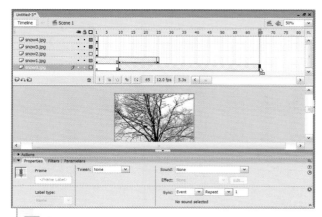

12 Click frame 65 of the snow0.jpg layer and press F5 to insert frames 10 to 65.

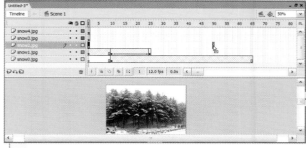

13 Move frame 1 of the snow2.jpg layer to frame 50.

14 Select frame 95 of the snow2.jpg layer and press F5 to insert frames.

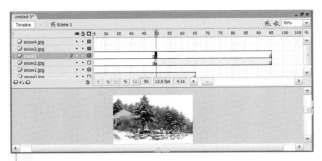

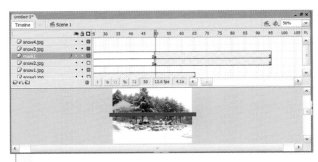

15 Select the snow2.jpg layer and click on the Insert Layer icon ( ) to insert a new layer. Name the layer "mask1". Select frame 50 and press F6 to insert a keyframe.

16 Using the Rectangle tool, draw a rectangle as shown here on the mask1 layer. Use the F8 shortcut key to register the rectangle as a movie clip symbol called "line."

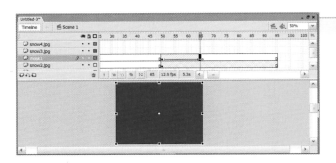

17 Select frame 65 of the mask1 layer and press F6 to insert a keyframe. Use the Free Transform tool to increase the size of the rectangle so that it is slightly larger than the Stage.

18 Insert a motion tween between frames 50 and 65. At frame 66, press F7 to insert a blank keyframe.

tip >>

Lines and Fills in Mask Layers

Objects on a mask layer determine what will show on the layers underneath, so when you draw on a mask layer, you can select any color. However, you must make sure that the shape has no lines, as these will be ignored in a layer mask and will show in the final animation.

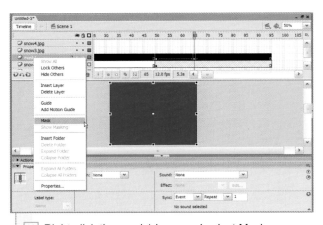

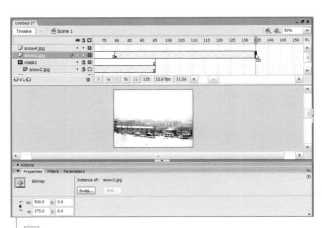

19 Right-click the mask1 layer and select Mask.

20 Select the snow3.jpg layer and drag frame 1 to frame 80. Click frame 135 and press F5 to insert frames.

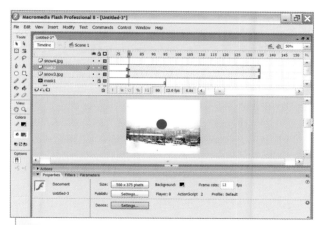

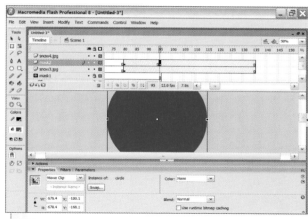

21 Select the snow3.jpg layer and click on the Insert Layer icon ( ) to add a layer. Name it "mask2." At frame 80, press F6 to insert a keyframe.

22 On the mask2 layer, use the Oval tool to draw a circle and register it as a movie clip symbol called "circle."

23 Insert a keyframe at frame 95 and use the Free Transform tool to increase the size of the symbol so that it is slightly larger than the Stage.

tip >>

Previewing Mask Effects

When a mask is created, the mask layer and the layers beneath it (that are masked) are locked. You can only preview a mask effect on the Stage when these layers are locked. Locking the layers has no effect on the published movie.

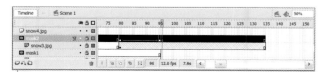

24 Insert a motion tween between frames 80 and 95. At frame 96, press F7 to insert a blank keyframe. Right-click on the mask2 layer and select Mask.

25 Move frame 1 of the snow4.jpg layer to frame 110. Select frame 150 and press F5 to insert frames.

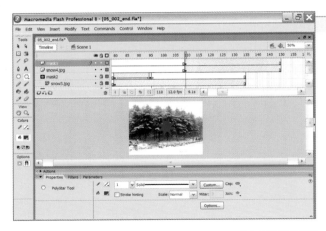

26 Select the snow4.jpg layer, click the Insert Layer icon (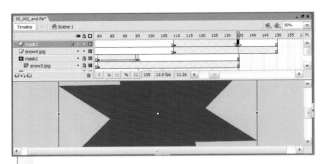) to insert a layer, and name it "mask3."

27 At frame 110, press F6 to insert a keyframe. Use the PolyStar tool to draw a small eight-pointed star as shown at left. Use the F8 key to convert the star to a movie clip symbol called "star."

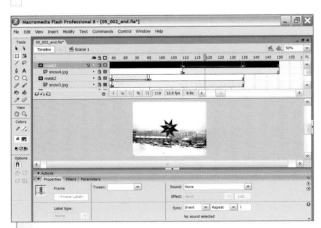

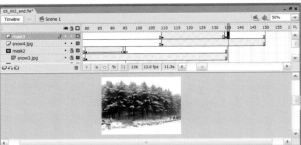

28 Insert a keyframe at frame 135. At frame 136, press F7 to insert a blank keyframe.

29 At frame 135, use the Free Transform tool to make the star larger than the size of the Stage, as shown.

30 Select the frames from 110 to 135 and create a motion tween. Right-click the mask3 layer and select Mask.

31 Press Ctrl-Enter (Command-Return for Macintosh) to preview your movie. You should see transitions between each set of still images.

tip >>

Increasing Size with the Alt/Option Key

If you hold down the Alt/Option key as you increase the size of an object, the size will increase evenly from the object's center.

3

Controlling a Movie with Behaviors

Behaviors provide an easy way to write ActionScript without having to open the Actions panel. In this example, you will use the Behaviors panel to add actions to Play and Stop buttons in a movie.

Start File
— 05_003.fla

Final File
— 05_003_end.fla

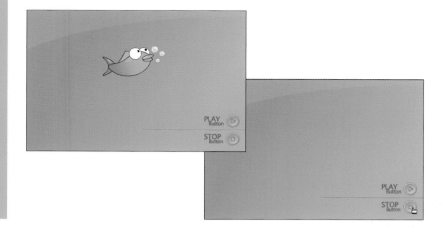

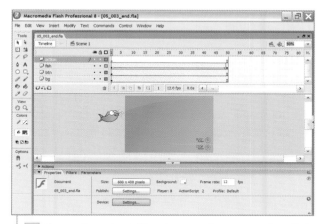

1. Open the start file; it contains a moving fish animation. Buttons to play and stop the animation appear in the bottom-right corner of the screen. Preview the movie by pressing Ctrl-Enter (Command-Return for Macintosh). Notice that the animation loops continuously without stopping.

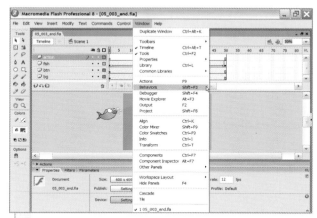

2. Select Window > Behaviors or use the shortcut Shift-F3 to open the Behaviors panel.

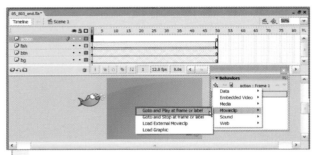

3 The animation should be paused at the beginning; we will control it using the Play and Stop buttons. Add a Goto and Stop action to frame 1 of the action layer by selecting the frame and clicking the Add Behavior icon ( ) in the Behaviors panel. From the menu, select Movieclip > Goto And Stop at frame or label.

4 In the "Goto and Stop at frame or label" dialog box, press OK to apply the default values.

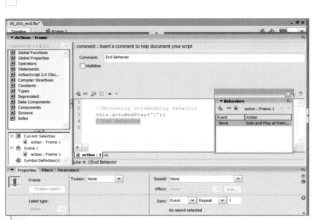

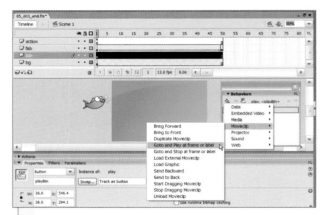

5 If you press F9 to open the Actions panel, you will see that a gotoAndStop() action has automatically been entered into frame 1 of the action layer. You will also see the action listed in the Behaviors panel.

6 Press Ctrl-Enter (Command-Return for Macintosh) to test the movie. The animation should be stopped.

7 Close the Actions panel by pressing F9. Select the Play button instance and use the Add Behavior button ( ) to select the Movieclip > Goto And Play at frame or label behavior.

8 Enter frame 2 at the bottom of the dialog box and press OK.

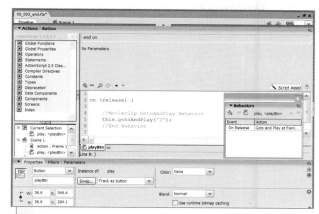

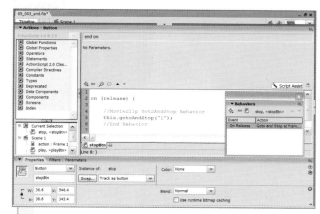

9 If you open the Actions panel, you will see that an On Release event has been added. When the Play button is clicked, the movie clip will move to frame 2 and play.

10 Close the Actions panel and select the Stop button. In the Behaviors panel, click the Add Behavior button ([⊕]) and choose Movieclip > Goto And Stop at frame or label. Press OK to accept the default values.

11 In the Actions panel, you will see an On Release event that moves to frame 1 and stops playing the movie.

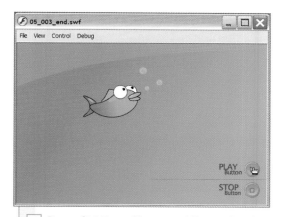

12 Press Ctrl-Enter (Command-Return for Macintosh) to test the movie. Click the buttons to make sure that the animation works correctly.

Using Behaviors to Control Movie Clips

In addition to controlling how buttons work, behaviors can be used to create draggable movie clips.

Start File
05_004.fla

Final File
05_004_end.fla

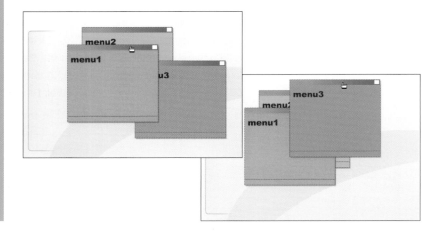

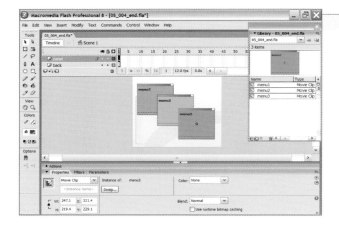

[1] The start file contains only a basic background design on the Stage. Press F11 to open the Library panel.

[2] Click frame 1 of the panel layer and drag the menu1, menu2, and menu3 movie clips onto the Stage, positioning them as shown here.

[3] In the Properties panel, enter "menu1_mc," "menu2_mc," and "menu3_mc" as instance names for each of the movie clips.

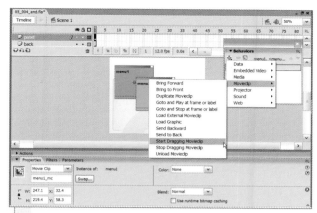

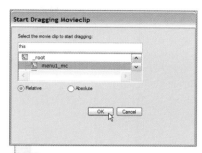

4 Let's make each of the movie clip instances draggable on the Stage. Select the menu1_mc movie clip instance, go to the Behaviors panel, and select Movieclip > Start Dragging Movieclip.

5 In the Start Dragging Movieclip dialog box, make sure that the Relative option is chosen and that menu1_mc is selected as the draggable movie clip instance. Click OK.

6 The Start Dragging Movieclip action needs to be applied while the mouse is held down on the panel. In the Behaviors panel, change the event to On Press.

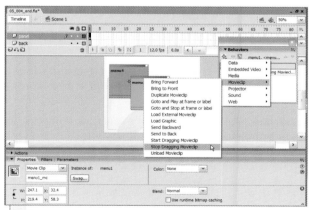

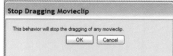

7 To stop the movement of the panel, select the menu1_mc movie clip instance and go to the Behaviors panel. Select Movieclip > Stop Dragging Movieclip and click OK.

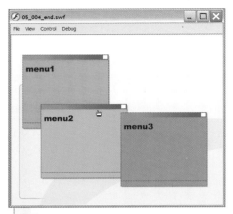

8 Repeat the steps above for the menu2_mc and memu3_mc movie clip instances.

9 Press Ctrl-Enter (Command-Return for Macintosh) to test the movie. Make sure you can drag each movie clip instance.

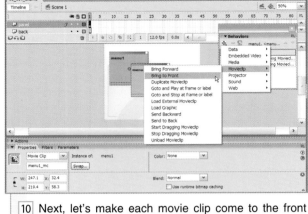

10 Next, let's make each movie clip come to the front when selected. Click the menu1_mc instance and select Movieclip > Bring to Front in the Behaviors panel.

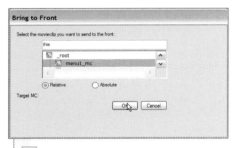

11 In the Bring to Front dialog box, make sure the Relative option and menu1_mc instance are selected. Click OK.

12 The Bring to Front action needs to be applied while the mouse is pressed on the button. In the Behaviors panel, change the Bring to Front event to On Press.

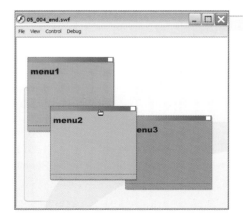

13 Repeat the steps above to define Bring to Front behaviors for the menu2_mc and menu3_mc movie clip instances. Make sure that the events for these two movie clip instances are changed to On Press.

14 Press Ctrl-Enter (Command-Return for Macintosh) to test the movie. When you drag each panel, it should move in front of the other panels.

Adding Actions to Frames and Buttons

In this exercise, you'll add Action-Script to control an animation. When the movie opens, the character in the animation will be stopped. Clicking a button will start the animation, and clicking another button will stop it. You achieved something similar in Exercise 3 using behaviors; this time you'll write the ActionScript code yourself in the Actions panel.

Start File
05_005.fla

Final File
05_005_end.fla

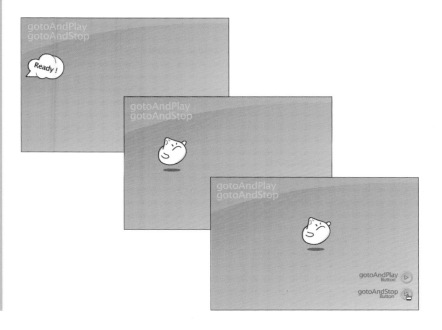

1 Open the start file. Press Ctrl-Enter (Command-Return for Macintosh) to test the movie. You should see the character moving across the Stage.

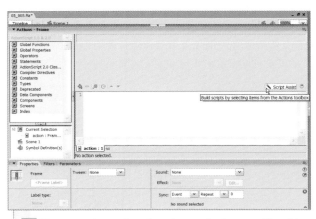

2 To stop the animation from playing, we'll add a stop() action at the beginning of the movie. Select frame 1 of the actions layer and press F9 to open the Actions panel. Make sure the Script Assist button is pushed in.

177

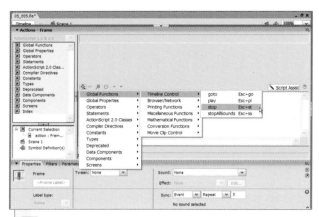

3 Click the Add Action button ( ) and choose Global Functions > Timeline Control > stop.

4 The Actions panel will show the stop() action in the keyframe at frame 1. This action stops the movie at frame 1.

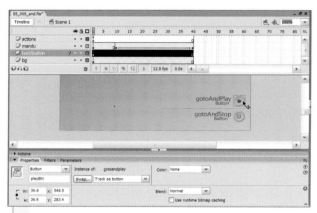

5 Close the Actions panel by pressing the F9 shortcut key. Press Ctrl-Enter (Command-Return for Macintosh) to test that the animation stops at frame 1.

6 Return to the movie and click the gotoAndPlay button instance on the bottom-right corner of the Stage.

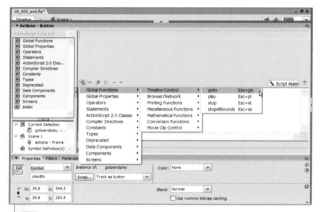

7 Open the Actions panel with the F9 key and choose Global Functions > Timeline Control > goto.

8 Enter 10 for the frame and leave the other options at their default settings.

9 The Actions panel will contain the code shown here. Because we selected a button before choosing the action, Flash has included an On Release handler. This means that the ActionScript lines inside the curly brackets will run when the user releases their mouse after clicking the button. In this case, the movie will advance to frame 10 and play.

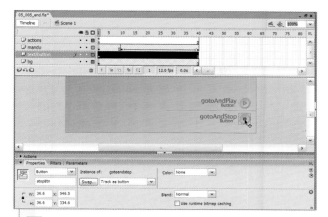

10 Press F9 to close the Actions panel, then select the gotoAndStop button at the bottom-right corner of the screen.

11 Open the Actions panel with the F9 key and choose Global Functions > Timeline Control > goto as you did with the previous button.

12 This time, click the Go to and stop option and enter 25 for the frame number.

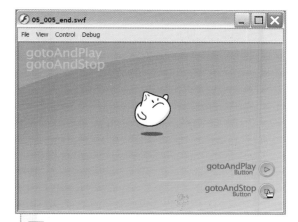

13 Again, Flash has added the On Release handler because we selected a button before adding the action. This time, when the user releases the button, the movie will go to frame 25 and stop playing.

14 Test the movie with Ctrl-Enter (Command-Return for Macintosh). You should be able to click the buttons to stop and start the animation.

6 Controlling Movie Clip Properties with ActionScript

In this example, you will learn how to change movie clip properties such as _xscale, _yscale, _rotation, _x, _y, and _alpha using ActionScript. We will create a movie in which buttons are used to change the properties of a movie clip instance.

Start File
05_006.fla

Final File
05_006_end.fla

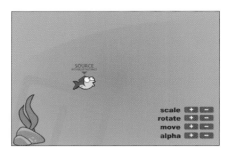

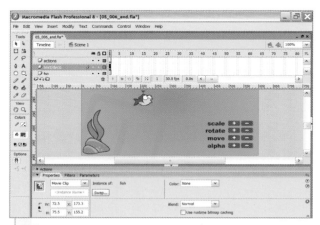

1 Open the start file. It contains a movie clip of a fish in an underwater setting. It also contains buttons titled "scale," "rotate," "move," and "alpha."

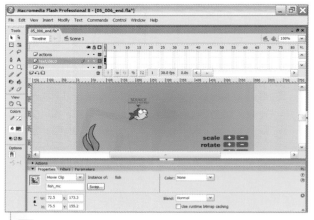

2 Select the fish movie clip from the Stage and enter the instance name "fish_mc" in the Properties panel.

tip >>

Get into the habit of naming each instance on the Stage. This is crucial when working with ActionScript. You can give names to buttons, movie clips, and some types of text fields. These names allow you to reference specific objects when writing ActionScript, so it is important that each name be unique.

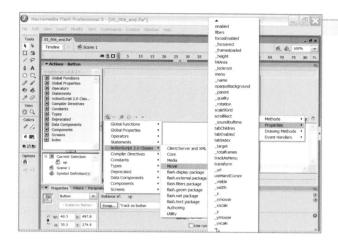

3 Select the Increase Scale button and press F9 to open the Actions panel.

4 Click the Add Action button and select ActionScript 2.0 Classes > Movie > Movieclip > Properties. Click the down arrow at the bottom of the properties list until you can see _xscale and click it to add it to the Actions panel.

5 You'll see the code shown here in the Actions panel. Flash has added an On Release handler for the button so that the ActionScript inside the curly brackets will run when the user releases the mouse. Inside the brackets is the line "not_set_yet._xscale."

6 Select the text "not_set_yet" in the Expression box at the top of the panel and click the Insert a target path button (⊕).

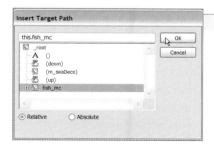

7 Choose the fish_mc instance name in the Insert Target Path dialog box. Leave the Relative option selected and click OK. The Expression box updates with the fish_mc instance name.

8 Modify the text in the Expression box to read "this.fish_mc._xscale +=10". This line will increase the size of the fish movie clip in the X direction by 10% each time the button is clicked.

9 Click on line 2 and choose ActionScript 2.0 Classes > Movie > Movieclip > Properties. Click the down arrow at the bottom of the properties list until you can see _yscale and click it to add it to the Actions panel.

10 Select the text "not_set_yet" in the Expression box at the top of the panel and click the Insert a target path button (⊕).

11 Choose the fish_mc instance name in the Insert Target Path dialog box. Leave the Relative option selected and click OK. The Expression box updates with the fish_mc instance name.

12 Modify the text in the Expression box to read "this.fish_mc._yscale +=10". This line will increase the size of the fish movie clip in the Y direction by 10% each time the button is clicked.

13 Test the movie with the Ctrl-Enter (Command-Return for Macintosh) shortcut. Check that you can increase the size of the fish movie clip with the Increase Scale button. Close the test movie.

14 Close the Actions panel and click the Reduce Scale button on the stage to select it. Open the Actions panel and repeat steps 4 to 13. This time your Expression boxes should read "this.fish_mc._xscale -=10" and "this.fish_ mc._yscale -=10".

tip >>

Toggling Script Assist Mode

You could also click the Script Assist button to turn it off and type the ActionScript code into the Actions panel yourself.

15 Test the movie and check that you can increase and decrease the size of the fish movie clip.

16 Choose the Rotate Increase button and repeat the steps above with the _rotation property. Make sure that the Expression box reads "this.fish_mc._rotation +=5".

17 Select the Rotate Decrease button on the Stage and repeat the steps, making sure that the Expression box reads "this.fish_mc._rotation -=5".

18 Test the movie and make sure that you can rotate the fish movie clip by clicking the buttons.

19 Select the Move Increase button and repeat the steps, choosing the _x property. When you've finished, the Expression box should read "this.fish_mc._x +=5".

20 Select the Move Decrease button and repeat the steps, again choosing the _x property. Alter the Expression box to read "this.fish_mc._x -=5".

21 Test the movie and make sure that you can move the fish movie clip to the left and right by clicking the buttons.

22 Select the Alpha Value Increase button and repeat the steps, choosing the _alpha property. This sets the transparency of a movie clip. When you're finished, the Expression box should read "this.fish_mc._alpha +=10".

23 Click the Alpha Value Decrease button on the Stage and repeat the steps to reduce the _alpha property. Make sure the Expression box reads "this.fish_mc._alpha -=10".

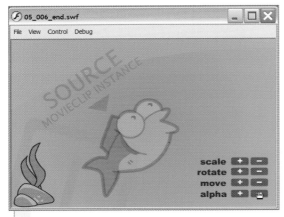

24 Test the movie and click the buttons to check that the fish_mc movie clip instance's properties change as expected.

Chapter | 6

Working with Sounds

So far, you have only learned to use Flash to create visual effects. As you will see in this chapter, Flash also offers many features for working with sound. You can greatly enhance your Flash movies by adding sound effects and background music, whether you create your own files or download copyright-free sounds from the Internet. However, sounds can dramatically increase the file size of a movie, so it is important to use them wisely.

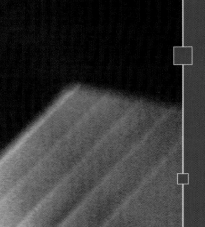

Importing a Sound File

L ike any other external file, sound is imported into Flash using the Import command. You can add a sound to the Library by selecting File > Import > Import to Library, choosing a sound file, and pressing OK. The sound will then be added to the Library.

Adding Sounds to the Library

Like any other external file, sound is imported into Flash using the Import command. You can add a sound to the Library by selecting File > Import > Import to Library, choosing a sound file, and pressing OK. The sound will then be added to the Library.

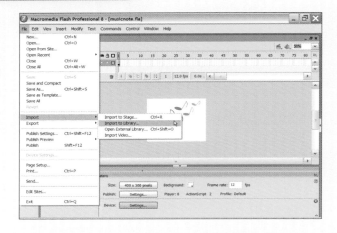

tip >>

Identifying Sounds in the Library

If you have imported a sound file, you should see the name of the file in the Library window with the word "Sound" next to it in the Type column.

Inserting a Sound File into a Movie

After you have imported a sound into the Library, you must add it to the movie before it will play. You can do this either by dragging the sound from the Library onto the Stage, or by selecting it from the Properties panel.

Using the Library to Insert Sounds

To add a sound to your movie, select a keyframe and drag the sound from the Library onto the Stage. The sound will then be inserted into that keyframe. You can tell that a frame contains sound when a blue waveform appears.

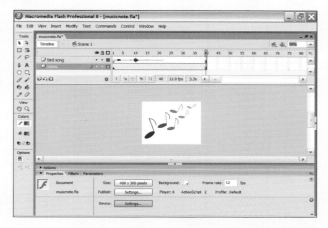

Using the Properties Panel to Insert Sounds

You can also use the Properties panel to add sound to your movie. Select the keyframe and choose the name of the sound from the Sound drop-down menu in the Properties panel.

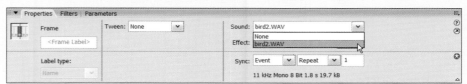

Removing a Sound

You can remove a sound from your movie either by using the Properties panel or by clearing the keyframe containing the sound.

Using the Properties Panel to Remove Sounds

To remove a sound using the Properties panel, select the frame where the sound has been added and set Sound to None.

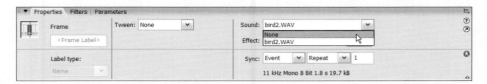

Using Keyframes to Remove Sounds

You can clear a sound from a keyframe by right-clicking the keyframe and selecting Clear Keyframe.

Deleting a Sound File from the Library

Removing a sound from the Timeline will not delete it from the Library. You can delete a sound by selecting it in the Library and clicking the trash can icon ( ). Sounds and symbols deleted this way cannot be recovered using the Undo command.

Sound Options

The sound options appear in the Properties panel.

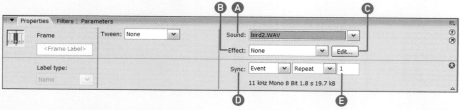

ⓐ **Sound**: Select a sound file from the Library.

ⓑ **Effect**: Effects for sound files, including fades and panning.

ⓒ **Edit**: Opens the Edit Envelope dialog box. You can use this to edit effects or change volume levels.

ⓓ **Sync**: Lets you choose how the sound will be played within the movie.
- **Event**: An event sound plays when the movie reaches a specified keyframe. The sound keeps playing until finished.
- **Start**: The Start option plays the sound when the keyframe plays. If no Stop option is included, Start works in the same way as Event.
- **Stop**: Stops the sound immediately when a specified keyframe is reached.
- **Stream**: If this option is selected, the sound will play as soon as the minimum amount of sound data has been transmitted, rather than waiting for the entire sound to load. The sound file is synchronized to the animation.

ⓔ **Repeat/Loop**: This is used to specify how many times the sound will loop or repeat. Looping is useful if you have a short sound file that you want to be played repeatedly throughout the movie.

Information about the recording settings for the selected sound file is displayed at the bottom-right corner of the panel.

Using Behaviors to Control Sound

There are five behaviors that you can use with sound files in Flash. You can use these behaviors to load a sound from the Library onto the Stage, load and play a streaming MP3 file, play a sound file, stop a sound file, or stop all sounds.

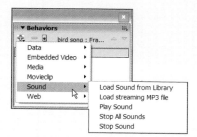

Some of these behaviors require a linkage name or instance name so that you can use Action-Script. A linkage name is a little like an instance name, as it allows you to specify a name for a Library symbol.

You can set a linkage name by right-clicking the sound instance in the Library and choosing Linkage.

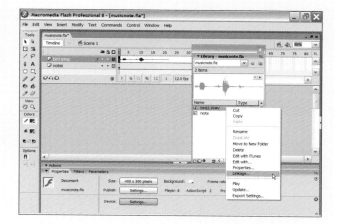

In the Linkage Properties dialog box, click the Export for ActionScript option, enter an Identifier, and click OK.

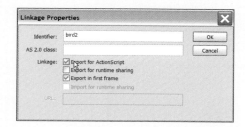

Behaviors for Use with Sound Files

Behavior	Purpose	Parameters
Load Sound from Library	Loads a sound from the Library using the linkage ID	Linkage ID in Library and sound instance name
Load streaming MP3 file	Loads and plays a streaming MP3 file	MP3 file name and path and sound instance name
Play Sound	Plays a sound instance	Sound instance name
Stop All Sounds	Stops all sounds that are currently playing	No parameters
Stop Sound	Stops a specified sound instance	Sound instance name

1 Adding Background Music

Background music can enhance the overall effect of a Flash movie. However, if you use an entire song as your background music, it will greatly increase the file size of the movie. One way to overcome this problem is to use a small sound loop that plays repeatedly. You can use a sound-editing program to create a loop or you can download a copyright-free sound loop from the Internet.

Start File
— 06_001.fla

Final File
— 06_001_end.fla

Import File
— sound1.mp3

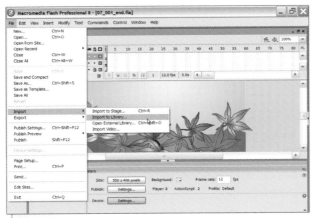

1 Open the start file and choose File > Import > Import to Library.

2 Select the sound1.mp3 file and press OK. The file will be imported into the Library. Open the Library with the Ctrl-L shortcut (Commmand-L on a Macintosh) to check that the sound file is there.

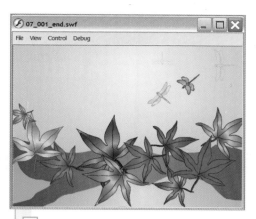

3 Click frame 1 of the sound layer and select sound1.mp3 from the Sound drop-down box in the Properties panel. Under Sync options, change Repeat to Loop.

4 Save the movie using the Ctrl-S shortcut, then press Ctrl-Enter to test it (Command-S and Command-Return for Macintosh, respectively). You should hear the background music playing (make sure you have your speakers turned on!). This freeware sound loop was created by Bernhard Kosten and was downloaded from Flash Kit (http://www.flashkit.com).

tip >>

Updating Sounds in the Library

If the sound file that you've imported changes, you can update it in Flash by right-clicking the sound in the Library and choosing Update. This will open the Update Library Items dialog box, which shows the items that need to be updated. Click the Update button to import the changed file.

Once the item has been updated, you can click the Close button.

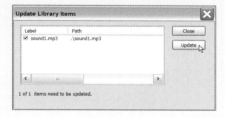

Exercise

2 Adding a Sound to a Button

Buttons are symbols that react to mouse actions. You can add sounds that play at various stages of a button being clicked—when the mouse is over the button, when the button is clicked, and when the mouse is away from the button. In this section, we will add sounds to each frame of the button Timeline.

Start File
06_002.fla

Final File
06_002_end.fla

Import Files
blip.mp3, click.mp3, dit.mp3

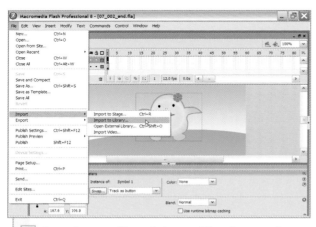

1 Open the start file and choose File > Import > Import to Library.

2 Click the files blip.mp3, click.mp3, and dit.mp3 while holding down the Ctrl/Command key and press Open.

3 Press Ctrl-L (Command-L for Macintosh) to view the sounds in the Library.

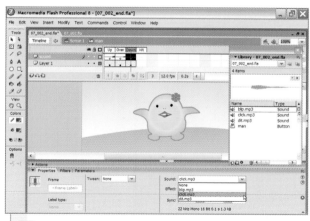

4 Double-click the man button on the Stage to enter symbol editing mode. Insert a layer above Layer 1 and name it "sound." Insert keyframes in the Over and Down frames by selecting them and pressing F6.

5 Select the Up frame and set the sound to dit.mp3 in the Properties panel. Set the Over frame to blip.mp3 and the Down frame to click.mp3.

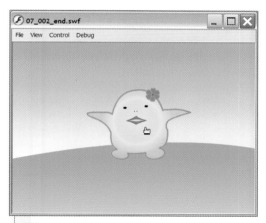

6 Press Ctrl-Enter (Command-Return for Macintosh) to test the movie. Move your mouse over and click the button to check that the sounds play as you interact with it.

Exercise

3

Using Sounds in an Animation

Sounds can be used in different ways in a movie: as background music, as button effects, and even for adding sound effects into your animations. In this example, we will add sound effects and background music to a movie.

Start File
06_003.fla

Final File
06_003_end.fla

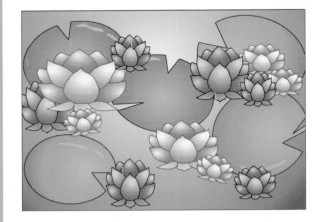

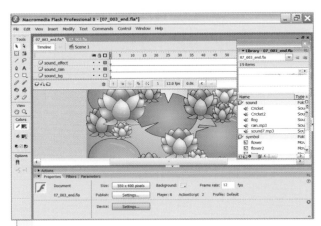

1 Open the start file. Press Ctrl-L (Command-L for Macintosh) and open the sound folder in the Library. You can see that this movie contains a number of sound files.

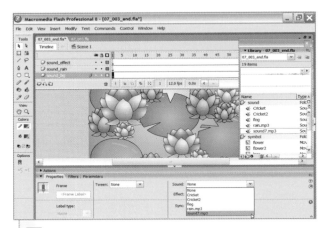

2 Click a frame in the sound_bg layer. In the Properties panel, set the sound to sound7.mp3 and sync to Start. You should see a blue line indicating that there is a sound in the sound_bg layer.

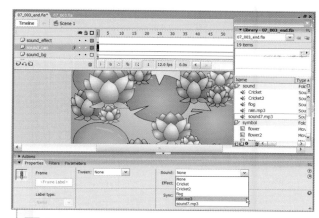

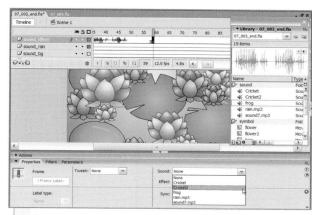

3 Select the sound_rain layer. In the Properties panel, set the sound to rain.mp3, set sync to Start, and change Repeat to Loop.

4 Select the sound_effect layer and add keyframes at frames 15, 35, and 59 with the F6 key.

5 Click on frame 15 and set the sound to Cricket in the Properties panel. Select frame 35 and set the sound to frog. In frame 59, set the sound to Cricket2.

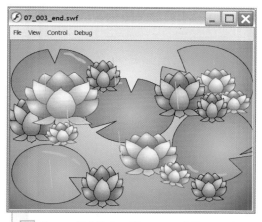

6 Press Ctrl-Enter (Command-Return for Macintosh) to test the movie. The background music is a freeware loop from calpomatt and was found at Flash Kit (http://www.flashkit.com).

Although background music can enhance a movie, it's a good idea to allow the user to turn it off if they wish. In this example, you will add a toggle button that turns the sound on and off in the movie.

Start File
06_004.fla

Final File
06_004_end.fla

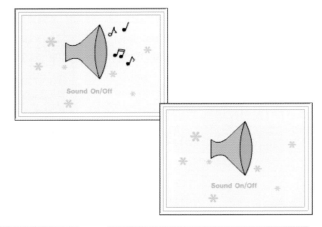

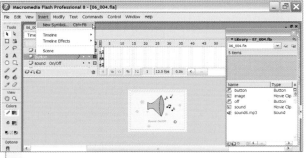

1 Open the start file and select Insert > New Symbol.

tip >>

New–Symbol Shortcut

The shortcut key to create a new symbol is Ctrl-F8 (Command -F8 for Macintosh).

2 Enter the name "sound," set the Type to Movie Clip, and click OK. You will be in symbol editing mode.

3 Click frame 1 and select sound6.mp3 from the Sound drop-down menu in the Properties panel.

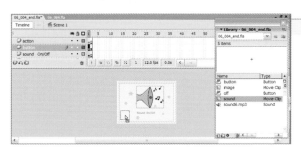

4 Click the Scene 1 button to return to the main Stage. Select frame 1 of the button layer and drag the sound movie clip from the Library onto the Stage. It doesn't matter where you drag the sound to, as long as it appears somewhere on the Stage.

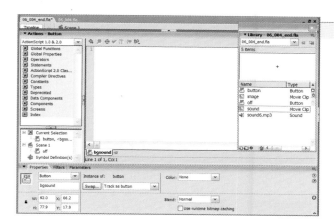

5 Select the button object in frame 1 of the button layer and open the Actions panel with the F9 shortcut key. Make sure that the Script Assist button is turned off. This time, you'll write the ActionScript yourself.

6 Enter the actions shown below in the Actions panel.

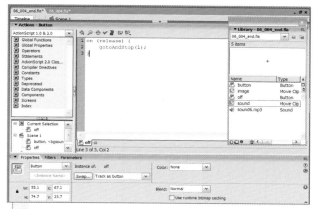

7 Close the Actions panel with the F9 shortcut key. Select the button object in frame 2 of the button layer and press F9 to open the Actions panel again. Enter the actions shown below.

Code	1 on (release) { 2 stopAllSounds(); 3 gotoAndStop(2); 4 }
Explanation	1 The actions will be triggered by the On Release event (i.e., releasing the mouse button). 2 Stop all sounds currently playing in the movie. 3 Go to frame 2 and stop playing the movie.

Code	1 on (release) { 2 gotoAndStop(1); 3 }
Explanation	1 Actions will be triggered by the On Release event (i.e., releasing the mouse button). 2 Go to frame 1 and stop playing the movie.

8 Press Ctrl-Enter (Command-Return for Macintosh) to test the movie. Click the button to make sure that the sound plays and stops as expected.

5 Making a Jukebox

In this example, we will create a jukebox that allows users to select the sound they want to hear or to turn off all sound in the movie.

Start File
06_005.fla

Final File
06_005_end.fla

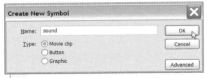

1 Open the start file and press Ctrl-F8 (Command-F8 for Macintosh) to insert a new symbol. Set the Name to "sound," set the Type to Movie Clip, and click OK.

2 You will now be in symbol editing mode. Insert keyframes at frames 2, 10, and 20 of the symbol's Timeline using the F6 key. Change the name of Layer 1 to "sound."

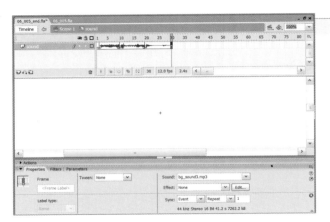

3 Using the Properties panel, add bg_sound1.mp3 at frame 2, bg_sound2.mp3 at frame 10, and bg_sound3.mp3 at frame 20. Use the F5 key to extend the animation to 30 frames.

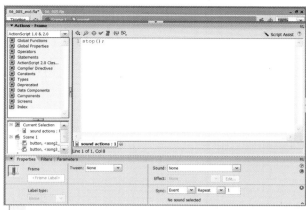

4 Insert a layer above the sound layer and call it "sound actions." Insert keyframes at frames 9, 19, and 30 with the F6 key.

5 Select frame 1 of the sound actions layer and press F9 to open the Actions panel. Make sure the Script Assist button is turned off and type "stop();" in the Actions panel. Repeat the process to add stop() actions in keyframes 9, 19, and 30.

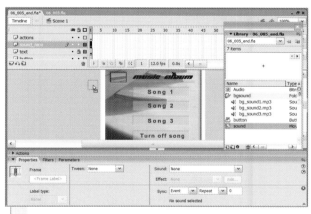

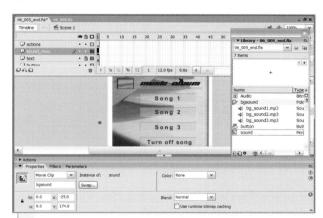

6 Close the Actions panel and click Scene 1 to return to the main Stage. Select frame 1 of the sound_mov layer and drag the sound movie clip from the Library into the movie. You can place it to the left of the Stage.

7 Select the sound movie clip and enter "bgsound" for the instance name in the Properties panel.

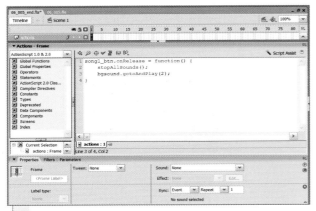

Code	1 `song1_btn.onRelease= function() {` 2 `    stopAllSounds();` 3 `    bgsound.gotoAndPlay(2);` 4 `}`
Explanation	1 Actions will be triggered by the On Release event of the song1_btn button instance (i.e., releasing the mouse after clicking the Song 1 button). 2 Stop all sounds playing in the movie. 3 Play frame 2 of the bgsound movie clip instance.

8 Select frame 1 of the actions layer and open the Actions panel. Enter the following code.

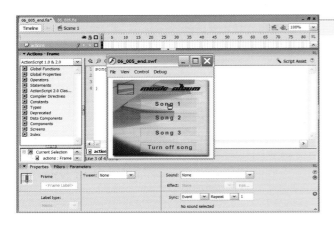

9 Test the movie using the Ctrl-Enter (Command-Return for Macintosh) shortcut. Click the Song 1 button to hear the first song play.

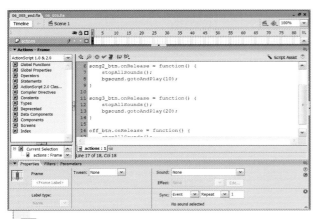

Code	1 `song2_btn.onRelease= function() {` 2 `    stopAllSounds();` 3 `    bgsound.gotoAndPlay(10);` 4 `}`
Explanation	1 Actions will be triggered by the On Release event of the song2_btn button instance (i.e., releasing the mouse after clicking the Song 2 button). 2 Stop all sounds playing in the movie. 3 Play frame 10 of the bgsound movie clip instance.

10 Close the window and enter the following code in the Actions panel.

Code	
| Code | ```
1 song3_btn.onRelease = function() {
2     stopAllSounds();
3     _root.bgsound.gotoAndPlay(20);
4 }
``` |
| Explanation | 1 Actions will be triggered by the On Release event of the song3_btn button instance (i.e., releasing the mouse after clicking the Song 3 button).
 2 Stop all sounds playing in the movie.
 3 Play frame 20 of the bgsound movie clip instance. |

Code	
| Code | ```
1 off_btn.onRelease = function() {
2     stopAllSounds();
3 }
``` |
| Explanation | 1 Actions will be triggered by the On Release event of the off_btn button instance (i.e., releasing the mouse after clicking the Turn off song button).
 2 Stop all sound playing in the movie. |

tip >>

Steamlining ActionScript

This time we've written the ActionScript code a little differently. Instead of placing the code inside each button instance, we've grouped it together on frame 1 of the actions layer and used slightly different commands. Keeping the code in one location is a good practice because it will make it much easier for us to find our code in the future.

11 Press Ctrl-Enter (Command-Return for Macintosh) to test the movie. You should be able to click the buttons to play different songs and to turn the music off completely.

Let's Go Pro!

Start File
06_006.fla

Final File
06_006_end.fla

Import Files
sound2.mp3, sound3.mp3

Using Behaviors to Control Sound

Behaviors can be used to control either Library sounds or external sound files. For example, you can use behaviors to play and stop external MP3 files in real time.

01 Open the start file. This file contains three buttons: buttons to play sound2 and sound3, as well as a button to stop all sounds.

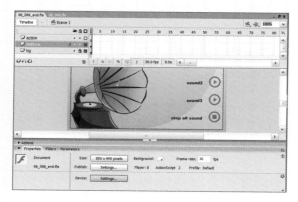

02 Open the Behaviors panel using the Shift-F3 shortcut. Click the sound2 play button. When we click this button, we want any current sounds to stop before we load the MP3 file. Click the Add Behavior button (△) and choose Sound > Stop All Sounds.

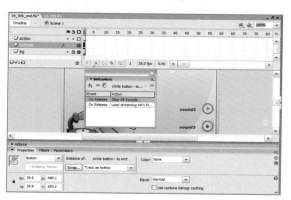

03 Click OK when you see the Stop All Sounds dialog box.

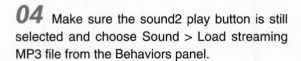

04 Make sure the sound2 play button is still selected and choose Sound > Load streaming MP3 file from the Behaviors panel.

05 Type "sound2.mp3" as the URL for the MP3 file to load. Enter "sound2" as the name for this sound instance. Click OK.

06 You should see two behaviors in the Behaviors panel. Click the Move Up button (⬆) so that the Stop All Sounds action appears at the top of the panel.

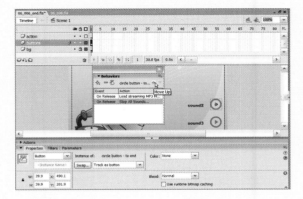

07 Click the sound3 play button. Add both the Sound > Stop All Sounds and Sound > Load streaming MP3 file behaviors from the Behaviors panel. Enter "sound3.mp3" for the sound URL and enter "sound3" for this sound instance name. Make sure that the Stop All Sounds action appears at the top of the panel.

08 Click the stop all sound button and add the Sound > Stop All Sounds behavior.

09 Press Ctrl-Enter (Command-Return for Macintosh) to test the movie. Click each of the buttons to hear their effects on the sound playing in the movie.

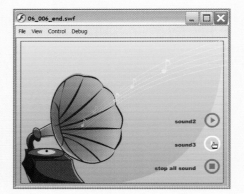

tip >>

Loading Your Own Sound Files

You can replace the MP3 files in this exercise with your own. Select the sound button on the Stage and double-click the Load streaming MP3 file behavior in the Behaviors panel.

This will open the Load streaming MP3 file dialog box and you can change the name of the MP3 file to one of your own.

Don't forget to copy the MP3 file to the same folder as the Flash file.

206

Chapter 7

Working with Video

Flash 8 offers many features for working with video clips. In addition, Flash Professional 8 includes a stand-alone software package called the Flash 8 Video Encoder, which you can use to convert existing video clips to FLV (Flash Video) format. This is Flash's own video format and it allows you to reduce the size of a video clip so that you can use it in your movies.

In Chapter 7 we'll cover some of the great things Flash 8 can do when you bring video to the party.

Embedding Video and Controlling Playback

As with sound, working with video primarily involves first adding it to your movies, and then determining how playback will function. After covering the basics, we'll jump right in to some video-heavy exercises.

Adding Video to Flash Movies

There are many different ways to add video to your Flash movies.

- Streaming the video using the Flash Communication server
- Progressively downloading the video from a Web server
- Importing embedded video
- Importing QuickTime video
- Importing FLV files

Video clips can quickly become very large in file size, and the most efficient way to use video in Flash is with the Flash Communication server. However, not everyone has the budget to use this approach. In this chapter, we'll focus on importing video. Note that when you import video into your Flash movies, it's best to use short video clips so viewers won't have to wait very long for the video to download; it's recommended that you only use videos that are less than 10 seconds long.

Embedding Video Clips

You can embed the following types of video in Flash:

- AVI
- DV
- MPEG
- MOV (requires QuickTime 7)
- WMV (requires DirectX 9 or later)

After you've embedded video, it will appear in the Timeline. You can also embed video into a movie clip. When you embed video into a Flash movie, you must make sure that the frame rates of the SWF and the clip match.

Because video files are so large, Flash includes two codecs (compressors/decompressors) that you can use to compress video: the On2 VP6 video codec that you'll use for publishing to Flash Player 8, and the Sorenson Spark Codec for Flash Player 7 and below. These codecs will compress video clips and reduce overall file size so that playback is quicker in Flash.

210

tip >>

Starting with Uncompressed Video

When you want to work with video, it's best to start with an uncompressed video clip. This will give you the highest quality movie in Flash.

Linking QuickTime Video

You have an additional option if you're working with QuickTime video clips. In this case, you can link to the QuickTime files rather than embedding them in your Flash movie. One important point is that you'll need to publish the Flash movie as a QuickTime file and target Flash Players 3 to 5.

You can choose File > Import and import the QuickTime file to the Library or Stage. This will start the Video Import Wizard; you'll need to specify Link to External Video File when asked how to deploy the video.

If you haven't set your publish settings appropriately in File > Publish Settings, you'll be prompted to do so.

You won't be able to preview the file by testing the movie. Instead, if you want to preview the movie, choose Control > Play.

Controlling Video Playback

There are several ways for you to control the playback of your video clips in Flash. You can:

- Add behaviors
- Use media components
- Write ActionScript to control video clips

Using Behaviors to Work with Embedded Video

You might do this if you want to create your own custom buttons to play and stop the video. Choose the Embedded Video section of the Behaviors panel to see the behaviors that generate actions to hide, pause, play, show, and stop a video clip.

Behavior	Explanation	Parameters
Hide	Hides the video	Instance name of the video clip to hide
Pause	Pauses the video	Instance name of the video clip to pause
Play	Plays the video	Instance name of the video clip to play
Show	Shows the video	Instance name of the video clip to show
Stop	Stops the video	Instance name of the video clip to stop

211

Using Media Components to Play Video Clips

If you've encoded an FLV file, you can use the FLVPlayback component to play, stop, and pause your video. If you use this component, you'll need to publish for Flash Player 8.

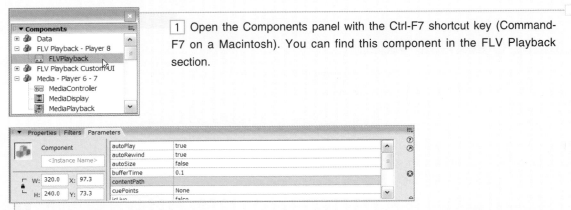

1 Open the Components panel with the Ctrl-F7 shortcut key (Command-F7 on a Macintosh). You can find this component in the FLV Playback section.

2 Next, drag the component onto the Stage and configure it using the options in the Parameters tab of the Properties panel. You can also change the size of the video using the Properties tab.

Parameter	Purpose
autoPlay	Plays the video automatically when the movie starts.
autoRewind	Rewinds the FLV file when it finishes playing or when the user stops the video.
autoSize	Resizes the component to the same size as the FLV file.
bufferTime	Sets the number of seconds of video to buffer before playback starts.
contentPath	Sets the path to the video file.
cuePoints	Sets the cue points for the movie so you can synchronize playback with other Flash elements.
isLive	Determines whether Flash is streaming from a Flash Communication server.
maintainAspectRatio	Determines whether to resize the player within the FLVPlayback component to retain the aspect ratio of the source FLV file.
skin	Sets the skin for the component.
skinAutoHide	Hides the skin when the mouse is not over the video.
totalTime	The total number of seconds in the FLV file.
Volume	Sets the volume, from 0 to 100.

Controlling Video with ActionScript

If you're working with an embedded video, you can control playback by using buttons to stop and start the Flash movie. Because each frame of the video corresponds to a frame in the Flash movie, stopping or starting playback of the main Timeline also stops and starts the video.

Exercise 1

Importing and Embedding Video Files

In this section, we'll work through an example to show you how to embed an AVI file in a Flash movie. Flash will encode the movie in Flash Video (FLV) format and place it on the Stage.

Final File
07_001_end.fla

Import File
sampleVideo1.avi

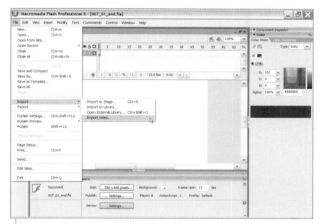

1 Create a new Flash file by choosing File > New and selecting the type Flash Document. Click the Size button in the Properties panel and enter a size of 320 by 240.

2 Choose File > Import > Import Video to start the Video Import Wizard.

3 Click the Browse button to select the video file to import.

4 Choose the file sampleVideo1.avi and click Open. Click Next.

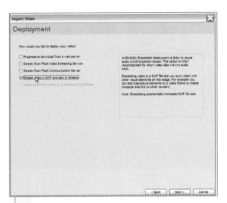

5 Choose the Embed video in SWF and play in timeline option and click Next.

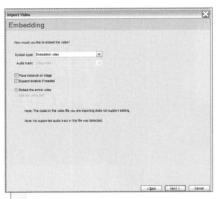

6 Leave the default options selected in the Embedding window and click Next.

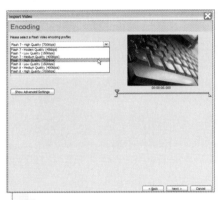

7 Choose an encoding method. In this case, we'll publish for Flash Player 7 at high quality. Because we're targeting Flash Player 7, Flash will use the Sorenson Spark codec to encode the video.

8 Click the Show Advanced Settings button to display the advanced options. Change the frame rate to Same as source and click Next.

9 Flash will display the message shown here. Click Finish to encode the video.

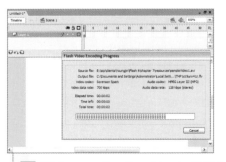

10 While encoding the video in FLV format, Flash will display an encoding progress window.

11 When the encoding is finished, you'll see the embedded video on the Stage and the Timeline will expand to show the length of the video clip.

12 Test the movie using the Ctrl-Enter (Command-Return for Macintosh) shortcut. You should see the video playing. You'll notice that the video repeats when it reaches the end.

Flash Video Format (FLV)

Flash Video format (FLV) is a video format specific to Flash. When you embed video using the Video Wizard, the clip is automatically encoded into FLV format. You can also import FLV files directly into the Library, without using the Wizard.

If you have Flash Professional, you can create FLV files using the Flash 8 Video Encoder. One advantage of doing this is that you can encode more than one file at a time, leaving you free to work on your Flash movies as batches of files are converted.

To encode video files using the Flash 8 Video Encoder:

01 Start the program and click the Add button to add a video clip to the encoder.

02 Navigate to the video file you wish to encode, select it, and click Open.

03 You can repeat the process to add more than one file.

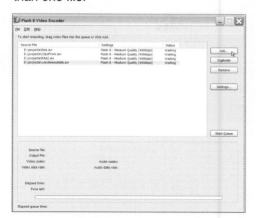

04 Click the Settings button to set the encoding options. You can choose how to encode the FLV file and set start and finish points for the video clip. You can also specify an output filename. Click the Show Advanced Settings button to see additional settings.

05 These options allow you to specify a codec, frame rate, quality, and audio settings. In addition, you can set cue points, and crop and trim the clip. When you're finished, click OK to return to the encoder.

06 Click the Start Queue button to start encoding the video clips.

07 Flash will encode the files in the list and save them in FLV format in the same directory as the original video clips. When the encoding has finished, you'll see the status of each video clip. You can then import the FLV files into your Flash movies.

2 Controlling a Video Clip with Behaviors

In this exercise, we will encode an FLV file and import it into a Flash movie. We'll use behaviors to add actions to buttons that will play, pause, stop, show, and hide the video. You'll only be able to complete this exercise if you have Flash Professional 8.

Start File
07_002.fla

Final File
07_002_end.fla

Import File
sampleVideo1.avi

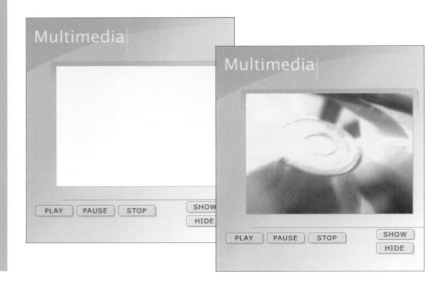

1 Open the Flash 8 Video Encoder.

2 Click the Add button and choose the sample Video1.avi resource file. Click Open.

3 Click the Start Queue button. The video encoder will start to encode the file.

sampleVideo1.flv
Flash Video File
567 KB

4 When the encoding is finished, close down the Flash 8 Video Encoder. You should see a new file, sampleVideo1.flv, saved with your resources.

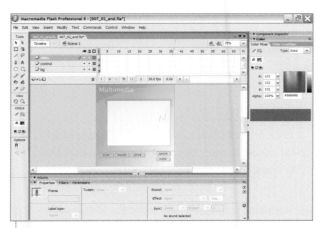

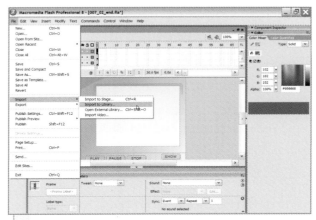

5 Open the start file. It contains play, pause, stop, show, and hide buttons that we'll use to control playback of the imported video clip.

6 Choose File > Import > Import to Library and select the encoded FLV file. This will start the Import Video Wizard.

7 Click Next and choose the Embed video in SWF and play in timeline option. Click Next.

8 Leave the default options selected and click Next.

9 You'll see the finish message. Click Finish.

10 Open the Library with the Ctrl-L (Command-L for Macintosh) shortcut. You should see the sampleVideo1.flv file listed.

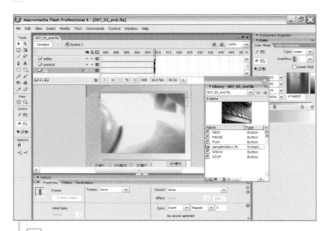

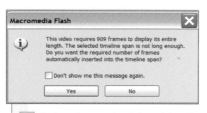

11 Select frame 1 of the video layer and drag the clip onto the Stage. When you see the warning shown here, click Yes to increase the number of frames in the Timeline.

12 Use the Properties panel to place the video at X: 57 and Y: 95. Select frame 909 of the control and bg layers and press the F5 button to add frames.

13 Select the video clip instance on the video layer and set the instance name to "sample_video" in the Properties panel. Close the Library panel.

14 The movie should stop at frame 1 so that the video clip doesn't play automatically. Open the Behaviors panel using the Shift-F3 shortcut. Select frame 1 of the actions layer and click the Add Behavior button (⊞). Choose Movieclip > Goto and Stop at frame or label.

15 Click OK to accept the default settings.

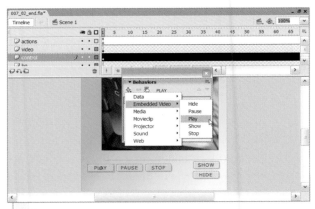

16 Select the Play button on the Stage and click the Add Behavior button (⊞). Choose Embedded Video > Play from the Behaviors panel.

17 Choose sample_video to specify the clip to play when the Play button is clicked. Click OK.

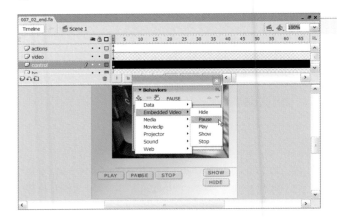

18 Select the Pause button on the Stage and add the behavior Embedded Video > Pause.

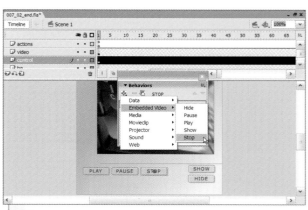

19 Choose sample_video and click OK.

20 Select the Stop button on the Stage and add the Embedded Video > Stop behavior.

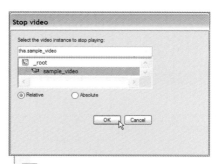

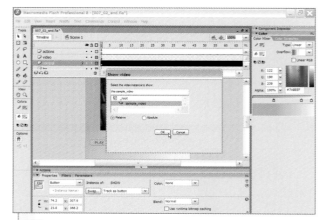

21 Select the sample_video instance and click OK.

22 Click the Show button on the Stage and add the behavior Embedded Video > Show. Choose sample_ video and click OK.

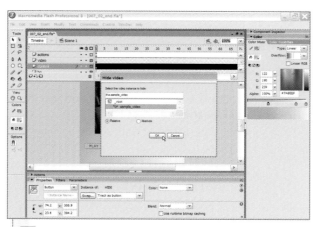

23 Select the Hide button and add the Embedded Video > Hide behavior, targeting the sample_video instance. Click OK.

24 Test the movie using Ctrl-Enter (Command-Return for Macintosh). Click each button to see the effect on the video clip.

3

Importing an FLV File Using Media Components

In this exercise, we'll use the FLVPlayback component to play an FLV file. This component automatically includes a control bar so viewers can start and stop the playback.

Start File
07_003_end.fla

Import File
sampleVideo2.flv

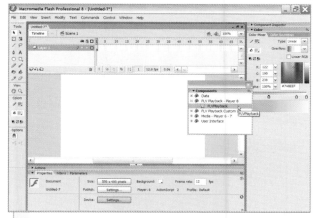

1 Create a new Flash document by choosing File > New and selecting Flash Document.

2 Open the Components panel using the Ctrl-F7 (Command-F7 for Macintosh) shortcut and drag the FLVPlayback component to the Stage.

3 Click the Parameters tab in the Properties panel and click the contentPath setting so that you can see a magnifying glass icon.

4 Click the magnifying glass icon to bring up the Content Path dialog box and then click the browse button, as shown.

223

5 Navigate to the sampleVideo2.flv file and click Open. Make sure the "Match source FLV dimensions" option is checked and click OK.

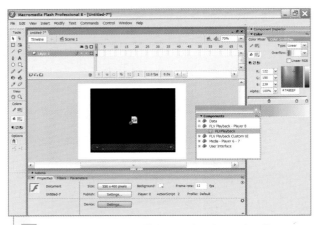

6 The component will be resized on the Stage to match the size of the FLV file.

7 Test the movie using Ctrl-Enter (Command-Return for Macintosh). You'll see the video playing and a semi-transparent control bar at the bottom of the window. Move your mouse over the pause button on the left to see it highlighted.

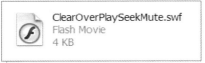

ClearOverPlaySeekMute.swf
Flash Movie
4 KB

8 If you check the published files, you'll see an additional file named "ClearOverPlaySeekMute.swf." This is the Flash movie that contains the video playback controls.

tip >>

Customizing the Control Bar

You can choose a different control bar by choosing a skin parameter in the Parameters tab of the Properties panel. The Select Skin dialog box allows you to choose from a number of preset control bars and shows a preview of each.

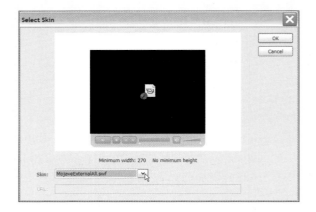

4

Controlling Playback with ActionScript

In this exercise, we'll create play, pause, and stop buttons to control the playback of a video clip. Instead of using behaviors, we'll write the ActionScript in the Actions panel using Script Assist.

Start File
07_004.fla

Final File
07_004_end.fla

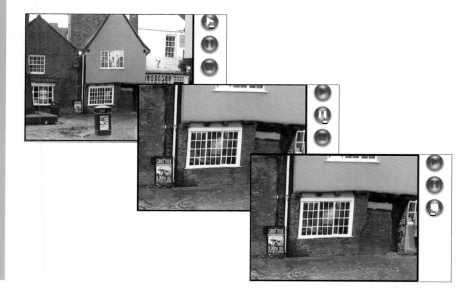

[1] Open the start file. You'll see an embedded video clip with three buttons to control playback.

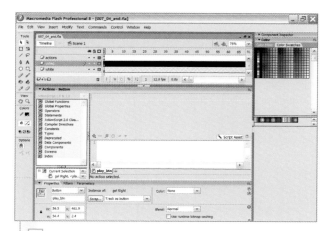

[2] Select the play button on the stage and open the Actions panel with the F9 shortcut key. Make sure the Script Assist button is pressed in.

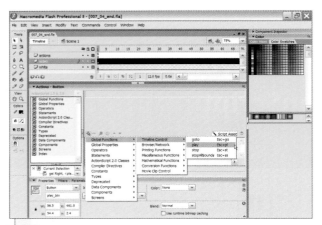

3 Click the Add New Item button () and choose Global Functions > Timeline Control > play.

4 The Actions panel should show the play() action as shown here.

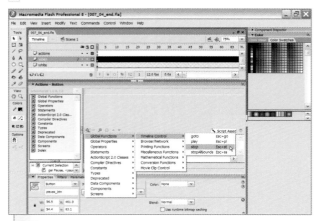

5 Close the Actions panel with the F9 key and select the pause button. Use the F9 key to open the panel again.

6 Add a new item and choose Global Functions > Timeline Control > stop.

7 The Actions panel should show a stop() action.

8 Close the Actions panel, select the stop button, and open the Actions panel again.

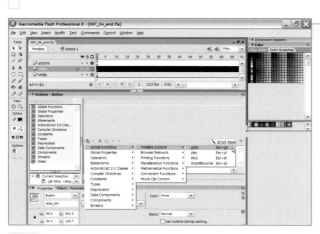

9 Add the item Global Functions > Timeline Control > goto.

10 Click the Go to and stop option and leave the other options at their default values. Close the Actions panel.

11 Test the movie with the Ctrl-Enter (Command-Return for Macintosh) shortcut. You should be able to click the buttons to control the playback of the video clip.

5

Importing a Linked QuickTime Video Clip

Instead of embedding a video in a Flash movie, you can link to a QuickTime clip. If you choose this approach, you'll need to change your publish settings to target Flash Players 3 to 5 and publish the file in QuickTime format.

Start File
07_005.fla

Final File
07_005_end.fla

Import File
1984.mov

EMBEDDED Q...

EMBEDDED Q...

EMBEDDED QUICKTIME

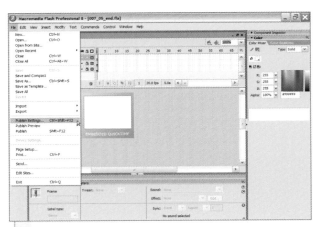

1 Open the start file and choose File > Publish Settings.

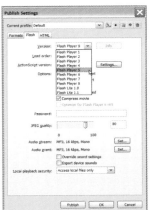

2 Switch to the Flash tab and change to Flash Player 5.

3 Click the Formats tab and deselect HTML. Check the QuickTime option and click OK.

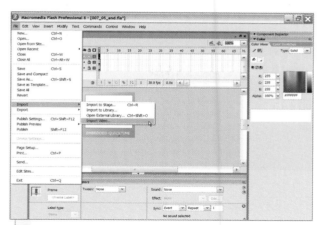

4 Select frame 1 of the video layer and choose File > Import > Import Video.

5 Click the Browse button and navigate to the 1984.mov file. Click Open and then Next.

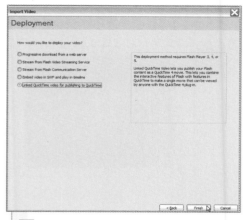

6 Make sure that the "Linked QuickTime video for publishing to QuickTime" option is checked and click Finish.

7 You'll be warned that the Timeline is not long enough to display the movie. Click Yes to add the required number of frames. Press F5 to increase the length of the control and bg layers to match.

8 In the Properties panel, position the movie at X: 20 and Y: 18.

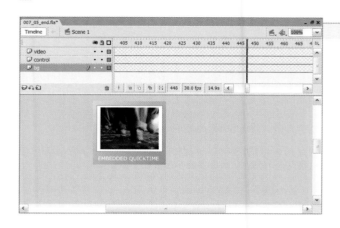

9 Test the movie by choosing Control > Play from the menu. You should see the movie play on the Stage.

10 Choose File > Publish to publish the movie.

6 Importing Video into a Movie Clip

Video can be imported into movie clip symbols so that you can add animation effects. One advantage of working this way is that each time the video movie clip symbol is duplicated, the file size of the Flash movie file will be unaffected. In this exercise, we will add a video clip to a movie clip symbol and apply some simple animation.

Final File
07_006_end.fla

Import File
sampleVideo3.flv

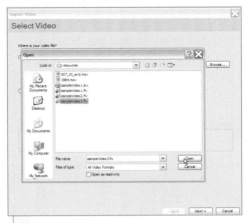

1 Create a new Flash document using File > New.

2 Choose File > Import > Import Video and browse to select the file sampleVideo3.flv. Click Open.

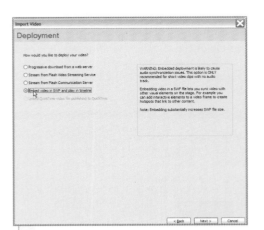

3 Click the Next button and select the Embed video in SWF and play in timeline option.

230

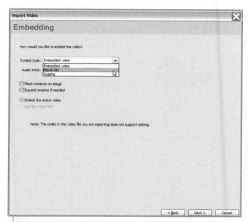

4 Click Next and choose movie clip as the symbol type. Leave the other options set at their default values and click Next.

5 When you see this message, click the Finish button.

6 You should see the embedded video on the Stage.

7 Press Ctrl-L (Command-L for Macintosh) to open the Library panel. You should see two symbols: the movie clip and the embedded video.

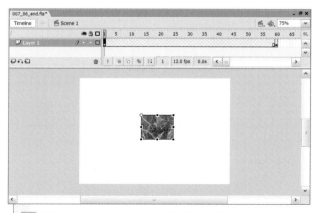

8 We'll add a simple animation that fades and resizes the movie clip. Click frame 60 and press F6 to insert a keyframe.

9 Click frame 1 and use the Free Transform tool to shrink and position the movie clip as shown.

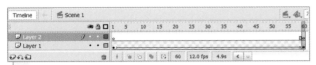

10 Add a new layer to the Timeline with the Insert Layer button (). Click on frame 60 and add a keyframe with the F6 key.

11 With frame 60 of Layer 2 selected, press F9 to open the Actions panel and make sure that the Script Assist button is selected. Choose Global Functions > Timeline Control > stop.

12 The Actions panel should show a stop() action.

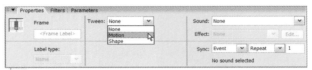

13 Close the Actions panel. Click frame 1 of Layer 1 and select a motion tween in the Properties panel. Leave the other settings at their default values.

14 Select the video clip instance at frame 1 and set the Color setting in the Properties panel to Alpha and the value to 0%.

15 Test the movie with the Ctrl-Enter (Command-Return for Macintosh) shortcut. You should see the video fade in and resize.

tip >>

Keeping the Video from Looping

To stop the video from repeating, you'll need to edit the movie to add a stop() action on the last frame.

Chapter 8

Creating Movies with Flash Lite

Flash Lite is a version of the Flash Player designed specifically for mobile phones. You can use Flash 8 to create Flash Lite movies that play on many common handsets. These movies can be anything from wallpapers and screensavers to games and complete player Flash Lite is a stripped-down version of the player, but you can still use many of the same features, such as movie clips, buttons, and ActionScript.

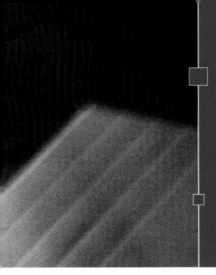

About Flash Lite

To begin, it's a good idea to familiarize yourself with the mobile devices that support Flash Lite; you you can find a complete list at http://www.adobe.com/mobile/supported_devices/. Each phone has different settings; before you start, you'll need to be aware of factors such as the size of the screen, the speed of the processor, how a user can interact with the phone (whether it has a touch screen, navigation buttons, etc.), and whether there's support for sound.

Getting Started with Flash Lite

Flash Professional 8 includes tools to help you to get started creating Flash Lite content for mobile phones. For instance, you can use the Flash Lite emulator to preview your content so you can see how it will look on a mobile phone's screen. Flash 8 also includes a number of templates to help you get started.

You can't use the components included with Flash in your Flash Lite movies. Instead, you need to download the Flash Lite Content Development Kit (CDK) from http://www.adobe.com/products/flashlite/. This kit includes special Flash Lite components, tutorials, and other resources.

Note that the Flash Lite Player doesn't come pre-installed on any devices, so if you want to test your movies on a supported device you'll have to buy the developer version by visiting http://www.adobe.com/products/flashlite/. Once you've created Flash Lite content, you'll have to transfer the movie to your mobile phone using infrared or Bluetooth, or by using the phone to download it from the Internet.

In late 2005, Macromedia (now owned by Adobe) released Flash Lite 2.0, which offers additional features such as ActionScript 2.0 support, video playback, and XML support. Flash 8 ships with Flash Lite 1.1 by default. At the time of this writing, authoring tools for Flash Lite 2.0 weren't available, so this chapter shows you how to work with Flash Lite 1.1.

http://www.adobe.com/products/flashlite/

236

ActionScript and Flash Lite

Flash Lite 1.1 uses the Flash 4 ActionScript engine. The actions that you write will look a little different from the current version of ActionScript (ActionScript 2.0), so you need to be aware of the following differences.

- When you use Flash Lite 1.1, you can't give instance names to buttons and text fields.
- You can't write ActionScript that post-dates the Flash 4 ActionScript standard, as it will not be recognized by Flash Lite 1.1.
- Mobile phones don't have a mouse, so you can't use the On Release event. Instead, you have to select the button and add your code inside a Press event handler, like this:

```
on (press) {
    //do some Flash Lite things
}
```

Getting Started

Flash 8 includes several Flash Lite templates to get you started. Choose File > New and click the Templates tab. You can select from the Global Phones and Japanese Phones categories.

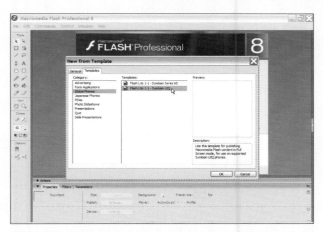

The Global Phones category allows you to create full-screen movies for the Symbian Series 60 and the Symbian UIQ group of phones. Choose this to target phones that are distributed worldwide. The Japanese Phones category is specifically aimed at phones in the Japanese market.

The best way to understand Flash Lite is to create a simple Flash Lite movie, which is what we'll do in Exercise 1. From there, we'll explore some of the other things Flash Lite can bring to your mobile phone.

1

Creating a Simple Flash Lite Movie

In this exercise, we'll create a very simple Flash Lite movie so you can see how the Flash Lite emulator works.

Final File
08_001_end.fla

1 Create a new Flash Lite movie by choosing File > New and clicking the Templates tab. You can also choose the template type from the Start Page. Choose the Global Phones type and select Flash Lite 1-1- Symbian Series 60.

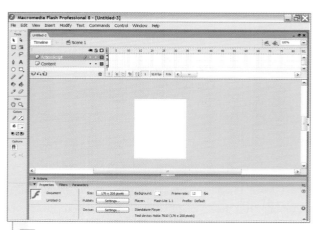

2 Click OK and you'll see a new movie sized to the correct dimensions and containing two layers: Content and ActionScript. The Properties panel shows the test device, which in this case is a Nokia 7610 phone.

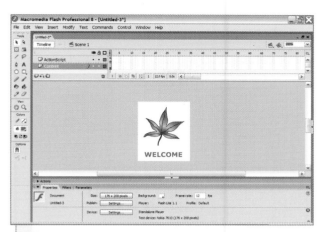

3 Select frame 1 on the Content layer and create a simple drawing like the one shown here on the Stage.

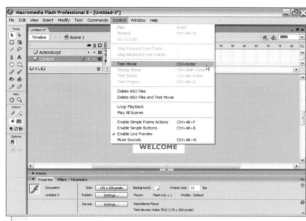

4 Test the movie in the Flash Lite emulator by choosing Control > Test Movie or by pressing Ctrl-Enter (Command-Return for Macintosh).

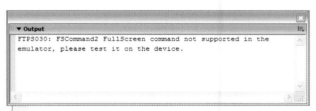

```
FTPS030: FSCommand2 FullScreen command not supported in the
emulator, please test it on the device.
```

5 You'll see any warnings specific to the device in the Output panel. You can click the X at the top-right corner to close this panel.

6 When you test the movie, you'll see that it looks quite different from other types of movies you've tested. You'll notice that the device appears on the right side and that there is a device emulation section on the left side.

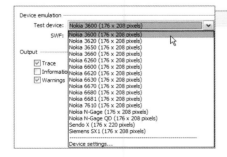

7 You can choose a different test device from the drop-down box at the top left of the screen.

8 After you've made your selection, the test movie will update with the new device and show any relevant warnings.

tip >>

Turning Off Device Warnings

If you don't want to see warnings about each device, uncheck Warnings in the Output section of the test movie.

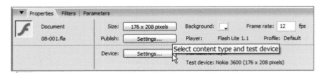

9 Close the test movie to return to the Stage. You can click the Settings button in the Properties panel to select other test devices.

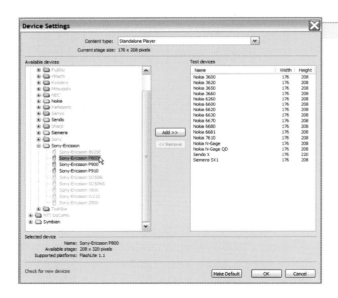

10 In the Device Settings dialog box, select a new test device. Click the Add button to add it to the list of test devices available in the emulator.

2

Creating a Mobile Phone Screensaver with Flash Lite

In this exercise, we'll use Flash Lite to create an animated screensaver for a mobile phone.

Start File
08_002.fla

Final File
08_002_end.fla

1 Open the start file. It was created from the Flash Lite 1-1-Symbian Series 60 template.

2 We'll start by adding our devices to the movie. Click the Stage to see the document properties in the Properties panel, then press the Settings button.

3 Choose Screen Saver from the Content type menu.

4 We'll target a Sony-Ericsson W21S phone, so select the Sony-Ericsson folder and click the Add button to add it to the list of test devices.

5 You'll notice that this device has a screen that is 240 x 320 in size. Click OK to return to the Stage.

6 Click the Size button in the Properties panel and enter a width of 240 pixels and a height of 320 pixels. Click OK.

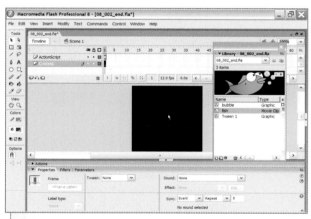

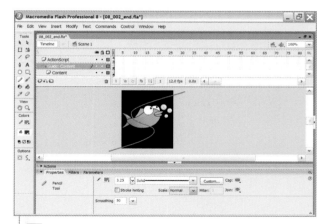

7 Now that we've set the target device, it's time to add the animation. Open the Library panel with the Ctrl-L (Command-L for Macintosh) shortcut. Click frame 1 of the Content layer and drag the fish symbol onto the Stage.

8 Close the Library panel. Click the Add Motion Guide icon (⬚) and use the Pencil tool to draw a motion guide path similar to the one shown here.

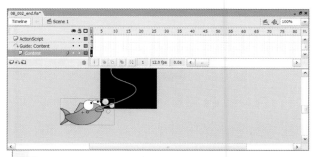

9 Align the fish symbol to the bottom-left of the guide.

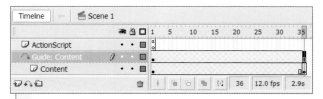

10 Insert a keyframe at frame 36 of the Content layer using the F6 key. Use the F5 key to add the same number of frames to the Guide: Content layer.

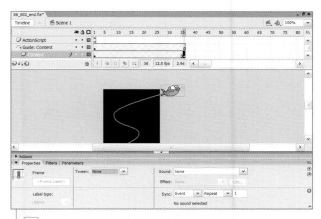

11 Select frame 36 of the Content layer and use the Transform tool to reduce the size of the fish symbol. Align it to the top right of the guide.

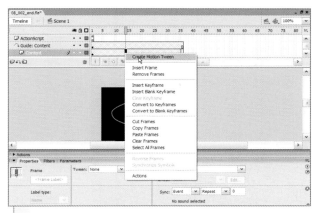

12 Right-click between frames 1 and 36 of the Content layer and choose Create Motion Tween.

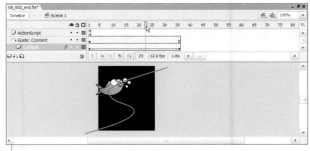

13 If you drag the Playhead across the Timeline, you should see the fish symbol move across the Stage following the motion guide.

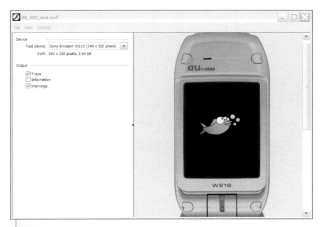

14 Test the movie and you should see the animation previewed on the Sony-Ericsson W21S.

3

Creating a Flash Lite Movie That Responds to User Input

In this exercise, we'll create a standalone Flash Lite movie that responds to user input. The user will be able to choose between two options that display different animations. The animations will load from external SWF files and the user will use the up, down, and select buttons to play the chosen animation.

Final File
> 08_003_end.fla

External Animations
> boy.swf, dragonfly.swf

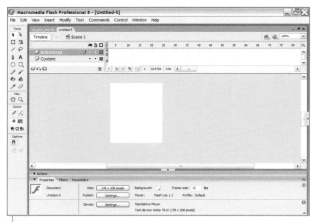

1 Create a new Flash movie by choosing File > New. Click the Templates tab and select Flash Lite 1-1-Symbian Series 60 from the Global Phones template. Check that the Standalone Player is selected in the Properties panel.

2 Click frame 1 of the Content layer and create a rectangle shape with rounded edges, as shown here. Choose any color that you like for the stroke and fill.

3 Select the shape and press F8 to convert it to a symbol. Call the symbol "button1" and select Button as the type. Click OK.

244

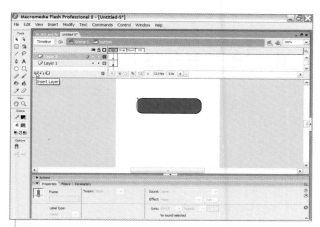

4 Double-click the button to edit it and click the Insert Layer button to add a new layer.

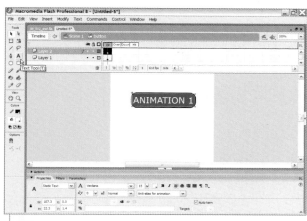

5 Use the Text tool to add the text "ANIMATION 1" on Layer 2.

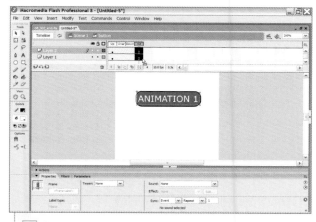

6 Select the Hit frame on both layers and use the F5 key to add frames.

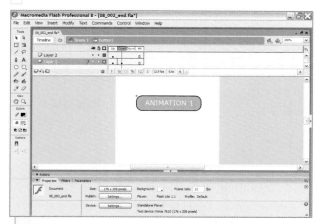

7 Add a keyframe to the Over frame on Layer 1 using the F6 key. Change the background color of the button.

8 Click Scene 1 to return to the Stage, then use the Ctrl-L (Command-L for Macintosh) shortcut to open the Library panel. Right-click the button1 symbol and choose Duplicate.

tip >>

Creating Buttons for Mobile Phones

When working with mobile phones, it's a good idea to create an Over state for your buttons so you can easily see which button has been selected on the mobile phone's screen.

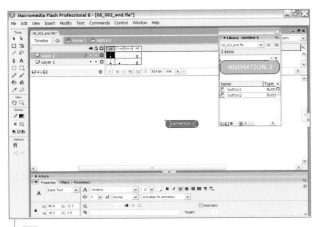

9 Enter the name "button2" and click OK.

10 Double-click the button2 symbol in the Library to enter edit mode. Change the text to read "ANIMATION 2" and click Scene 1 to return to the Stage.

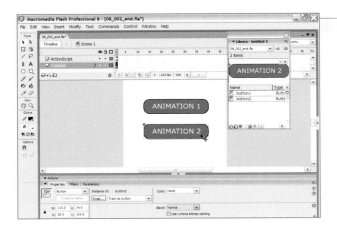

11 Drag button2 from the Library and place it under the button1 instance.

12 The user will use the Up and Down arrow keys on the phone to select an option. Once a button is selected, they will see its Over state. Clicking the button will load one of two external Flash files. Save the Flash movie in the same location as the boy.swf and dragonfly.swf files.

13 Before we can add ActionScript to the buttons, we'll need to add a stop() action to frame 1 and create an empty movie clip to hold the external animation files for the buttons. Select frame 1 of the ActionScript layer and press F9 to open the Actions panel.

14 Making sure the Script Assist button is not pushed in, click at the end of line 2 and press Enter. Type the text "stop();" and press F9 to close the Actions panel.

15 Click frame 10 of the Content layer and press the F7 key to add a blank keyframe. Press Ctrl-F8 (Command-F8 for Macintosh) to create a new symbol. Enter the name "empty" and select Movie Clip as the type. Click OK and then click Scene 1 to return to the Stage.

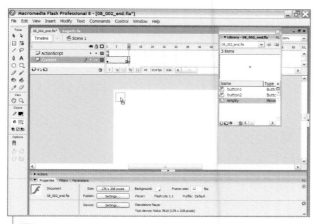

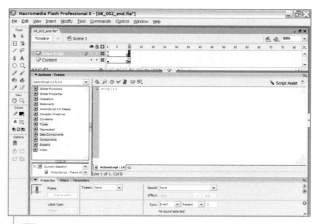

16 Drag the empty movie clip to the top left of the Stage. Use the Properties panel to place it at X: 0, Y: 0 and name it "empty_mc." We'll use this movie clip as a holder for the external animation files that we load. Close the Library panel.

17 Click frame 10 of the ActionScript layer and add a keyframe with the F6 key. Open the Actions panel with the F9 key and add a stop() action as shown here.

Code	
| | ```
on(press) {
    gotoAndStop(10);
            loadMovie("boy.swf",
"empty_mc");
}
``` |

Code	
| | ```
on(press) {
    gotoAndStop(10);
      loadMovie("dragonfly.swf",
"empty_mc");
}
``` |

18 Close the Actions panel and click frame 1 of the Content layer. Select the ANIMATION 1 button and open the Actions panel again. Enter the above code; this code moves the movie to frame 10 and loads the animation called boy.swf into the empty_mc movie clip.

19 Close the Actions panel and click frame 1 of the Content layer. Select the ANIMATION 2 button and open the Actions panel again. Enter the above code; this code moves the movie to frame 10 and loads the dragonfly.swf animation into empty_mc.

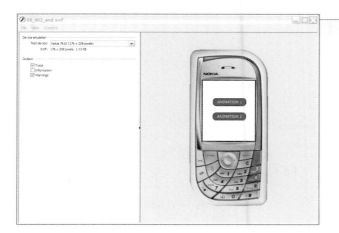

20 Close the Actions panel and test the movie. You should see something similar to the image shown here.

21 Click the down key to select the ANIMATION 1 button.

22 The button will appear in its Over state. Notice the yellow square around the button.

23 Click the Select button in the center of the navigation keys to play the first animation.

24 You should see the animation play.

25 When the animation finishes, you'll notice that there's no way to get back to the first frame of the movie. We'll need to add another button to frame 10 so that we can go back to frame 1 and select a different animation.

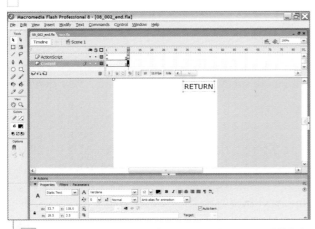

26 Close the test movie (and the Actions panel if it is still open). Click frame 10 of the Content layer and use the text tool to add the text "RETURN."

27 Press the F8 key to convert it into a button symbol called "return." Click OK.

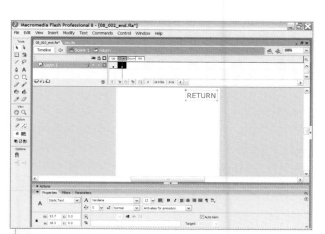

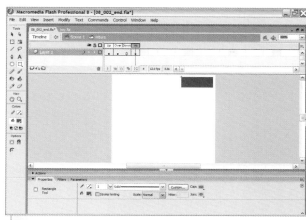

28 Double-click the symbol to edit it and add a keyframe to the Over frame with the F6 key. Select the text in this frame and change the color.

29 Press F5 to add a Down frame and then F6 to add a Hit keyframe. Draw a box over the text in the Hit frame. The color isn't important, but the box will define the selection area for this button.

Code	`on (press) {`
	`    gotoAndStop(1);`
	`}`

30 Click Scene 1 to return to the Stage. Select the button and open the Actions panel with the F9 key. Enter the code shown here; these actions tell Flash to return to the first frame and stop.

31 Test the movie again. Choose the first animation. This time you should be able to use the up button on the emulator to select the RETURN Flash button.

tip >>

Remove Highlight from Emulator Buttons

You probably noticed a yellow box around your buttons when you tested the file in the Flash Lite emulator. You can remove this by adding the following action to frame 1 of the ActionScript layer:

```
_focusRect = false;
```

32 When you click the select button, you should return to the first frame of the movie.

33 Test that you can choose both buttons to load the animation files. You can add the movie to a device that supports Flash Lite using Bluetooth, infrared, or a USB cable, or by allowing the phone to download it from the Internet.

Updating the List of Target Devices

Since new mobile phones are released all the time, it's a good idea to periodically update the list of target devices that Flash Lite can recognize. You can do this by downloading an extension from the Device Profiles Update Web site. You'll need to install the Extension Manager from the Adobe website at http://www.adobe.com/ exchange/em_download/ before you can update the list.

01 Make sure you're working with a Flash Lite document and click the Settings button in the Properties panel.

02 Click the "Check for new devices" link to download new devices from the Web site.

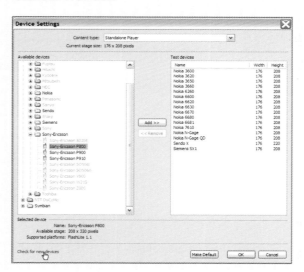

03 This will display the Device Profile Updates page. You can click the "Download now" link to download the latest mobile device profiles.

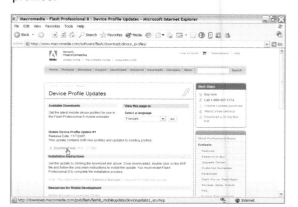

04 When prompted, click the Save button and choose an appropriate location.

05 Close the Device Settings dialog box and double-click the device update file that you downloaded in the previous step. You'll be asked to click the Accept button to proceed.

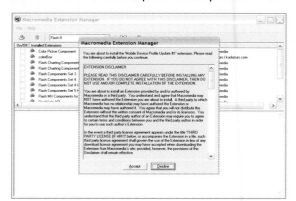

06 When you're finished, you'll see the following message. Click the OK button.

07 You'll see a list of device profiles that have changed.

08 Close the Extension Manager and shut down Flash. When you restart Flash, the list of devices will be updated.

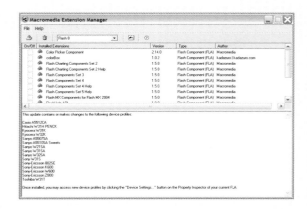

Chapter | 9

It's a Wrap!

So far, you've been previewing and testing your movies in Flash. Before you publish a movie, however, you'll need to optimize it by considering issues such as your audience, the final destination for your Flash movie, and the size and structure of your movie files. In this chapter, you will learn to optimize a movie, use the Bandwidth Profiler to check if the movie will load properly at different connection speeds, and finally, to publish a Flash Player file and an optional HTML file.

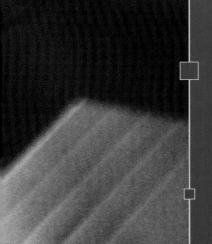

Optimizing a Movie

For a Flash movie to reach a wide audience over the Internet, it is important to keep the file size small. There are a number of ways to optimize a movie in order to reduce file size.

Optimizing Objects

The first thing to consider is how objects are used in the movie. If an object is used more than once, it should be registered as a symbol in the Library. Symbols are loaded only once in each movie regardless of the number of times that they appear on the Stage. Each instance of the symbol can have different settings such as size, color, and position on the Stage.

You should also group your objects wherever possible, as it reduces the workload for the Flash Player. You can do this by choosing Modify > Group or using the Ctrl-G shortcut (Command-G on a Macintosh).

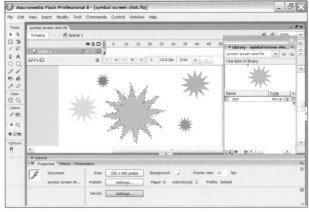

Reusing symbols from the Library

Optimizing Color

Gradients are more complicated to process than solid colors, so you should minimize the number of gradients that you use in your movies. Using alpha transparencies can also make your movies run more slowly. When you are working with many fade effects in a movie, you'll create smaller movies if you tween brightness values rather than alpha values.

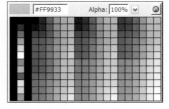

254

Optimizing Lines

Your choice of line style can also affect the size of your published movies. Solid lines take up less room than non-solid lines, as shown here.

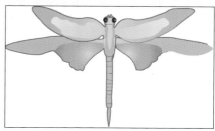

Solid line file size: 2 Kilobytes

Dashed line file size: 6 Kilobytes

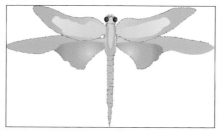

Dotted line file size: 18 Kilobytes

Optimizing Curves

You can also reduce file size by simplifying any vector images that you import into Flash. Break apart images using the Ctrl-B shortcut (Command-B on a Macintosh) and optimize the curves by choosing Modify > Shape > Optimize.

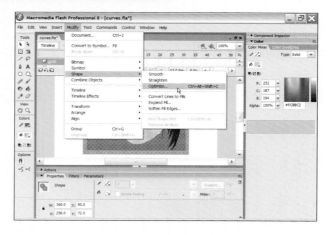

The Optimize command removes unnecessary curves from the image and can reduce the overall size of the file. Bear in mind, however, that overusing the Optimize command can distort the original shape.

Optimizing Text

One way to optimize text is with anti-aliasing, which softens the text edges and gives letters a smoother appearance. Flash 8 allows you to select different types of anti-aliasing for your text from the Properties panel.

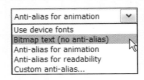

Keep in mind that when you use a font in a Flash movie, it is embedded in the SWF file. Using a large number of font faces and font styles can add unnecessary size to your published movie. You should also avoid breaking apart fonts unless necessary, as this will add to the movie's size.

Here the text "Flash 8" is shown in different fonts.

Optimizing Bitmap Images

Flash works best with vector images, so avoid using bitmaps unless they are necessary for your movie. Each time you include a bitmap image, you will add size to your movie.

You should avoid animating bitmaps, because Flash stores one copy of the image in each frame of the animation. If possible, trace the bitmap to convert it into a vector image.

Whenever you use a bitmap in Flash, it should be compressed.

Compressing Individual Bitmap Images

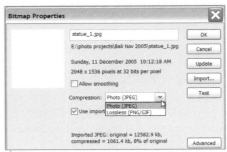

1 You can select the compression settings for an image by right-clicking the image in the Library and choosing Properties from the shortcut menu.

2 In the Bitmap Properties dialog box, choose the type of compression that you want to apply from the Compression drop-down box.

Compressing All Bitmap Images

You can compress all the bitmap images in a movie using the same settings by selecting File > Export > Export Movie and using the slider to change the value for JPEG quality. As you decrease the value, both the file size and the image quality will be reduced.

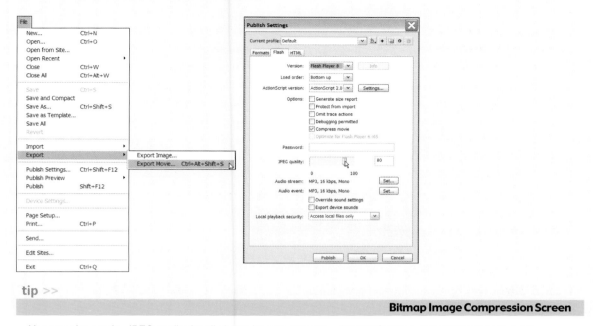

Bitmap Image Compression Screen

tip >>

You can also set the JPEG quality for all photos by selecting File > Publish Settings and clicking the Flash tab.

Optimizing Sound Files

Sound files can greatly increase the size of your Flash movies. Using short sound loops for background music can help to minimize the file size. If you are sampling your own sounds, use the lowest bit depth and sample rate that gives you acceptable quality.

When possible, you should use MP3 files instead of WAV or other formats, as MP3s have a much higher compression rate. You can also compress sounds in Flash by changing compression settings for a single sound or for all sounds within the movie.

Compressing Individual Sounds

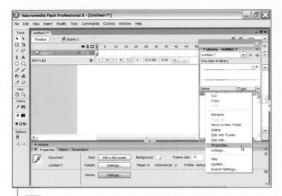

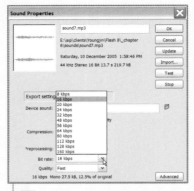

1 To compress a sound, right-click the sound file's name in the Library and select Properties.

2 In the Sound Properties dialog box, select the compression settings you want. You can also change the Bit rate and Quality settings.

Compressing All Sounds

You can apply the same sound compression settings to all sounds in a movie by selecting File > Publish Settings. Choose the Flash tab and click the Set button to edit the Audio stream and Audio event options.

You can then make changes in the Sound Settings dialog box.

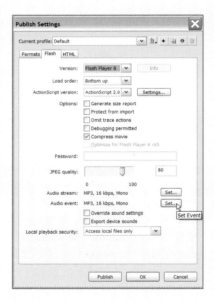

Optimizing Animations

Use tweened animations wherever possible, as they take up less file space than frame-by-frame animations. Also, try to limit the amount of change that happens in each frame; animating several objects at the same time or creating animations that contain large changes can affect the speed at which the movie runs.

Limit Modify Shape Commands

The Convert Line to Fills, Expand Fill, and Soften Fill Edges commands in the Modify > Shape drop-down menu should only be used where necessary, as they increase file size and slow down animation.

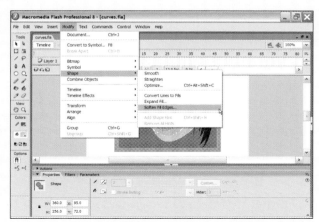

Delete Unnecessary Content

You can also reduce file size by deleting unnecessary content, such as:

- All blank or unnecessary frames and keyframes
- Empty layers
- Unused objects inside layers

Using the Bandwidth Profiler

There are several ways to test how your Flash movie loads before it is published. One way is to use the Bandwidth Profiler, which shows how well a Flash movie has been optimized. It is useful in determining whether the movie will load correctly at different Internet speeds.

If your movie is complex, you might want to stop it from playing until all the frames have been loaded. This is called preloading, and it will ensure that playback is smooth. To keep the user's interest, you can create an animation as part of the preloading.

To open the Bandwidth Profiler, first test the movie with the Ctrl-Enter (Command-Return for Macintosh) shortcut. Select View > Bandwidth Profiler from the Test Movie window.

You will see the Bandwidth Profiler window, as shown here.

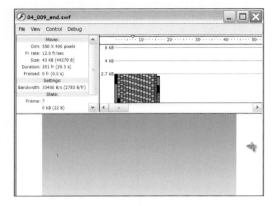

The Bandwidth Profiler Window

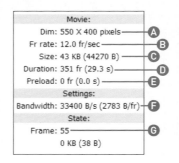

A Dim: The movie's dimensions

B Fr rate: The frame rate in frames per second

C Size: The movie's file size in KB (Kilobytes)

D Duration: The total number of frames and total duration of the movie

E Preload: How long it takes to load the movie at the current bandwidth

F Bandwidth: The number of bytes of data that are transmitted per frame

G Frame: The size of the selected frame and object

Bandwidth Profiler Graphs

The Bandwidth Profiler allows you to see two different types of graphs that can help you identify which parts of your movie are likely to cause downloading problems. The red line in the middle of each graph shows the limits of the selected download speed. Areas above the red line are frames where the movie may have to pause to download before playing.

The Streaming Graph

Usually, the first part of the movie is downloaded and played while the rest of the frames are loaded in the background. The streaming graph shows the frames in which the loading takes place. Choose View > Show Streaming to show the streaming graph.

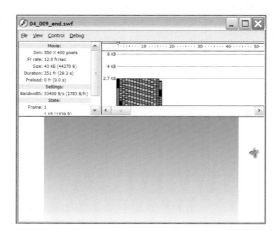

The Frame-by-Frame Graph

The frame-by-frame graph displays the size of each frame and is useful for determining which frames may cause the loading of the movie to slow down. Choose View > Frame By Frame Graph to show this graph.

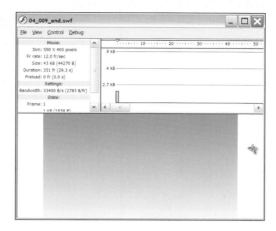

Simulating Download Time

When people view your Flash movie on a Web page, the speed of the Internet connection will determine how smoothly the movie plays. It is important to identify the likely Internet connection speeds of your audience and tailor the movie accordingly.

You can simulate different download speeds to test how long it takes for the movie to be loaded. Select View > Download Settings and choose a download speed. You can then watch the movie download at that speed by selecting View > Simulate Download.

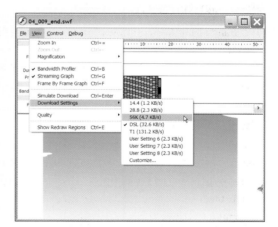

Publishing a Movie

Each time you press Ctrl-Enter (Command-Return for Macintosh) to test your Flash movie, you compile a SWF file of the movie. You can preview the SWF file in Flash or double-click it to view it in the Flash Player. When you are satisfied with your movie you'll want to publish it. Publishing the movie allows you to create numerous support files in addition to the SWF, such as an HTML page, a static image, a QuickTime movie, or a standalone Flash Projector file. Select File > Publish or use the shortcut Shift-F12 to publish your files.

Publish Settings

Publishing outputs Flash movies in different file formats. You can decide how to publish a file by selecting File > Publish Settings and choosing options from the Publish Settings dialog box.

You can also access the publish settings through the Properties panel. Click outside the Stage and the Properties panel will display the document properties. Click the Settings button to open the Publish Settings dialog box.

Publishing Formats

The Formats tab of the Publish Settings dialog box allows you to choose the formats that you'd like to use for your movie. Each time you check a format type's checkbox, another tab will be added to the Publish Settings dialog box. The tab contains the publishing options for that file type.

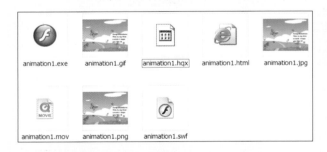

Selecting the published file types

Creating Flash Player (SWF) Files

When you select Flash as a published file type, the Flash setup options appear in the Publish Settings dialog box.

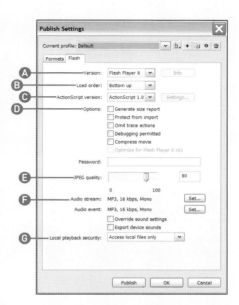

Ⓐ Version: Enables you to select a Flash Player version between Flash Player 1 and Flash Player 8.

Ⓑ Load order: Determines the order in which the layers of the first frame will be loaded.

- Bottom up: Loads from the bottom layer upwards.
- Top down: Loads from the top layer downwards.

Ⓒ ActionScript version: Enables you to choose between ActionScript 2.0 and ActionScript 1.0.

Ⓓ Options

- Generate size report: Movie information is generated as a TXT file.
- Protect from import: Stops others from importing the SWF file into Flash.
- Omit trace actions: When the test movie is run, this option suppresses any ActionScript Trace actions.
- Debugging permitted: The published movie can be debugged in a Web browser.
- Compress movie: Compresses the SWF file. This option is always set on by default and is available for Flash Player versions 6 and later.
- Optimize for Flash Player 6 r65: This option appears only when the Version is set to Flash Player 6. It is used to optimize for the Flash Player 6 r65.

Ⓔ JPEG quality: Sets the amount of compression used to compress bitmap images in the movie.

Ⓕ Audio stream and Audio event: These options are used to set the compression levels for all streaming and event sounds in the movie. If "Override sound settings" is not checked, individual sound settings in the Library will override the general settings.

Ⓖ Local playback security: Determines whether the published file can access only local files or network files as well.

Generating HTML

The Publish feature can also be used to generate an HTML page that displays the SWF file on the Web. Select File > Publish Settings and check the HTML option. When you publish the movie, an HTML file will be created.

The published SWF and HTML files

tip >>

What Is HTML?

HTML, or Hypertext Mark-Up Language, is the language used to write documents that are viewed in a Web browser. An HTML document is composed of a set of tags that determine how information appears on a Web page.

Displaying a Flash movie in Internet Explorer

1

Generating SWF Files with the Export Movie Command

When a movie is published, the FLA file will be saved along with an SWF file of the same name. You can alter the publish settings to generate an SWF file with a different name. You can also save the SWF file in a different location if you use the Export Movie command.

Start File
09_001.fla

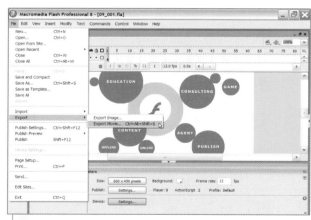

1 Open the start file and choose File > Export > Export Movie.

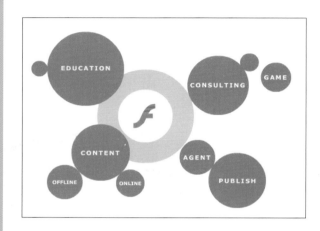

2 In the Export Movie dialog box, enter "Solution" as the filename and choose a save location for the file. Click Save.

3 In the Export Flash Player dialog box, accept the default properties for the SWF file and click OK.

4 The SWF file will be created. You can double-click the file to view it in the Flash Player.

Creating a Full-Screen Movie for a CD-ROM

When creating Flash movies for CD-ROMs, there are two things you need to keep in mind. First, the movies need to be created as EXE files so that they can be played on any PC, regardless of whether or not the Flash Player is installed. Second, most Flash movies made for CD-ROMs need to play in full-screen mode. In this example, you will learn how to make a full-screen EXE file that can be played on any PC.

Start File
└ 09_002.fla

Final File
└ 09_002_end.fla

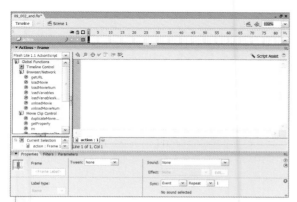

[1] Open the start file and save it to your hard drive. Select frame 1 of the action layer and press F9 to open the Actions panel.

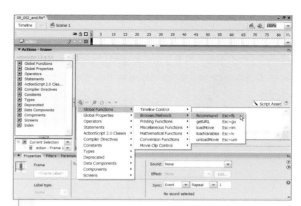

[2] Make sure that the Script Assist button is pressed in and add the Global Functions > Browser/Network > fscommand action.

3 Type "fullscreen" in the Command field and "true" in the Parameters field.

4 Choose File > Publish Settings and check Windows Projector (.exe) in the Format tab. This will create a projector file suitable for a PC. You can check Macintosh Project (.hqx) to create a file for a Macintosh computer. Click Publish and then OK.

09_002_end.exe
Macromedia Flash Player 8.0 r22
Macromedia, Inc.

5 You will see that an EXE or HQX file has been created in the folder where the original Flash movie was saved. Double-click the file to view the movie on your computer.

6 You should see a full-screen movie. Press Esc to return the movie to its original size.

7 Burn the EXE or HQX file to a CD to create a standalone Flash movie.

Creating a Transparent Flash Movie

In this example, we'll publish a Flash movie with a transparent background so that it uses the background color of the Web page in which it's viewed.

Start File
09_003.fla

Final File
09_003_end.fla

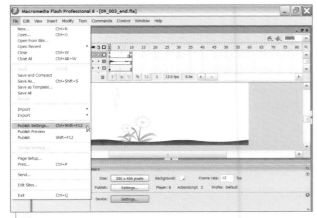

[1] Open the start file and save it to your hard drive. Choose File > Publish Settings.

[2] Make sure the HTML file type is checked and select the HTML tab. Click the Window Mode drop-down menu and select Transparent Windowless. Press the Publish button at the bottom and then click OK.

09_003_end.html
HTML Document
2 KB

09_003_end.swf
Flash Movie
81 KB

[3] You should see that an HTML document and an SWF file have been created in the folder where the original Flash movie was saved.

267

4 Double-click the HTML file and a Web browser window will open. If you are using Internet Explorer, select View > Source to see the HTML code.

tip >>

| Inserting Flash Movies into Dreamweaver |

If you are going to insert a transparent Flash file into Dreamweaver, you don't need to create the HTML page using Flash. Instead, include the code "wmode = "transparent"," along with the name of the Flash file to be inserted.

```
<html xmlns="http://www.w3.org/1999/xhtml" xml:lang="en" lang="en">
<head>
<meta http-equiv="Content-Type" content="text/html; charset=iso-8859-1" />
<title>09_003_end</title>
</head>
<body bgcolor="#000000">
<!--url's used in the movie-->
<!--text used in the movie-->
<!-- saved from url=(0013)about:internet -->
<object classid="clsid:d27cdb6e-ae6d-11cf-96b8-444553540000"
codebase="http://fpdownload.macromedia.com/pub/shockwave/cabs/flash/swflash.c
<param name="allowScriptAccess" value="sameDomain" />
<param name="movie" value="09_003_end.swf" />
<param name="quality" value="high" />
<param name="wmode" value="transparent" />
<param name="bgcolor" value="#ffffff" />
<embed src="09_003_end.swf" quality="high" wmode="transparent"
bgcolor="#ffffff" width="550" height="400" name="09_003_end" align="middle"
allowScriptAccess="sameDomain" type="application/x-shockwave-flash"
pluginspage="http://www.macromedia.com/go/getflashplayer" />
</object>
</body>
</html>
```

6 To check that the movie is transparent, change the line below...

```
<body bgcolor="#ffffff">
```

... so that it reads:

```
<body bgcolor="#000000">
```

```
<html xmlns="http://www.w3.org/1999/xhtml" xml:lang="en" lang="en">
<head>
<meta http-equiv="Content-Type" content="text/html; charset=iso-8859-1" />
<title>09_003_end</title>
</head>
<body bgcolor="#ffffff">
<!--url's used in the movie-->
<!--text used in the movie-->
<!-- saved from url=(0013)about:internet -->
<object classid="clsid:d27cdb6e-ae6d-11cf-96b8-444553540000"
codebase="http://fpdownload.macromedia.com/pub/shockwave/cabs/flash/swflash.c
<param name="allowScriptAccess" value="sameDomain" />
<param name="movie" value="09_003_end.swf" />
<param name="quality" value="high" />
<param name="wmode" value="transparent" />
<param name="bgcolor" value="#ffffff" />
<embed src="09_003_end.swf" quality="high" wmode="transparent"
bgcolor="#ffffff" width="550" height="400" name="09_003_end" align="middle"
allowScriptAccess="sameDomain" type="application/x-shockwave-flash"
pluginspage="http://www.macromedia.com/go/getflashplayer" />
</object>
</body>
</html>
```

5 The HTML source contains the line shown here, which is the HTML code that makes the movie transparent.

7 Choose File > Save to save the HTML file.

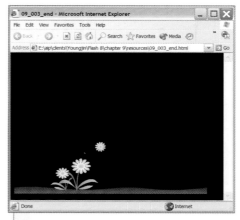

8 Click your browser's refresh button. You will see that the background color has changed to black and the Flash movie is transparent.

Let`s Go Pro!

Start File
09_004.fla

Final File
09_004_end.fla

Matching the Flash Movie Size to the Window Size

When you create a Flash movie, you can set the height and width of the Stage. In this exercise, you'll set up the movie to automatically match the size of the window in which it is shown.

01 Open the start file and select File > Publish Settings.

02 Click the HTML tab and choose Percent from the Dimensions drop-down menu. Make sure that the Scale is set to Default (Show all). Press the Publish button and then click OK.

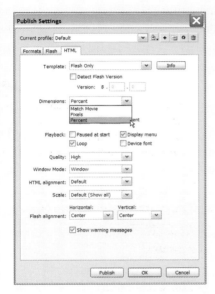

03 Double-click the HTML file that has been created and change the size of your browser window. You will see that the movie scales to match the size of the browser window.

Index > > >